JACQUES LECOQ
AND THE BRITISH THEATRE

Routledge Harwood Contemporary Theatre Studies
A series of books edited by Franc Chamberlain,
University College Northampton, UK

Please see the back of this book for other titles in the Contemporary Theatre
Studies series

JACQUES LECOQ
AND THE BRITISH THEATRE

edited by
Franc Chamberlain
University College Northampton, UK
and
Ralph Yarrow
University of East Anglia, UK

London and New York

First published 2002
by Routledge
11 New Fetter Lane, London EC4P 4EE

Simultaneously published in the USA and Canada
by Routledge
29 West 35th Street, New York 10001

Routledge is an imprint of the Taylor & Francis Group

© 2002 Taylor & Francis

Typeset by Scientifik Graphics (Singapore) Pte Ltd
Printed and bound in Great Britain by Biddles Ltd, Guildford
and King's Lynn

British Library Cataloguing in Publication Data
A catalogue record for this book is available from the British Library

Library of Congress Cataloging in Publication Data
A catalogue record for this book has been requested

ISBN 0-415-27024-3 (hbk)
ISBN 0-415-27025-1 (pbk)

Cover illustration: Bouge-de-là Theatre. Photo: Al Cane.

CONTENTS

INTRODUCTION TO THE SERIES

Contemporary Theatre Studies is a book series of special interest to everyone involved in theatre. It consists of monographs on influential figures, studies of movements and ideas in theatre, as well as primary material consisting of theatre-related documents, performing editions of plays in English, and English translations of plays from various vital theatre traditions worldwide.

Franc Chamberlain

LIST OF PLATES

PREFACE

The material for this volume was already to hand before the death of Jacques Lecoq in January 1999. I believe Lecoq never received the recognition that he deserved in the English-speaking world and this book, as the first collection of essays in English to focus on his work, aimed to rectify the situation.

Rather than attempting to sum up Lecoq's career or contribution as a completed project, the authors write of their engagement with Lecoq as a dialogue with the work of a living master whose practice was continuously shifting and changing, a process rather than a closed system.

Death, through its finality, causes us to pause and reflect on a life as a whole, it tempts us to fix a set of practices as the authentic contribution of a teacher, losing the sense of the living openness of the approach. Jacques Lecoq's work will live on through the creativity of his students and their ability to make theatre vital.

I greatly regret that this volume was not published whilst Lecoq was alive, but I am pleased to have been free from the temptation to make this the 'definitive' book on Lecoq. It is a contribution to a conversation that has barely begun . . .

Franc Chamberlain

1

INTRODUCTION

Franc Chamberlain and Ralph Yarrow

This volume does not set out to review the effects of Jacques Lecoq's teaching everywhere. His school has been in operation for over forty years and companies of ex-students have flourished around the world. In focusing on the influence of his work in Britain, the essays here however inevitably bring out key features of his approach which are relevant to performers and companies everywhere; they raise questions about the relationship of his pedagogy to drama training and about the ways in which performers, companies, directors, writers/devisers and audiences who have experienced the work incorporate it into their practices and expectations and thus contribute to changing the nature of theatre.

In what follows immediately, Franc Chamberlain sets out some personal parameters to the encounter with Lecoq on the British theatre scene. This is followed by a summary of the approaches of the essays in this volume which places them in other contextual frames.

From the Bakery to the National

In the autumn of 1974 I was working a Friday-night shift at a bakery whilst studying for my A-levels. My local Little Theatre, The Loft in Leamington Spa, was hosting a weekend mime workshop with Geoffrey Buckley.[1] I remember turning up on the Saturday morning straight from work wearing a black surplus National Fire Service greatcoat, covered in acne, with my skin feeling an unpleasant mixture of grease and flour. My eyelids felt as though they had flour underneath them, which they probably did. My memory of my arrival is still quite strong because I always felt slightly out of place in the theatre and felt particularly self-conscious about my appearance having not slept since the Thursday night. I think I remember someone commenting on my commitment …

It was during this workshop that I first heard the name Jacques Lecoq. Because Buckley focused on *pantomime blanche* during the weekend, however, Lecoq's name became equated in my mind with Marceau-type images of imaginary staircases, windows, invisible barriers and so on. Buckley's performance on the Sunday evening involved him attempting to speak to the audience but being prevented from being heard by an imaginary glass barrier, like an invisible safety curtain. He would struggle to lift the obstacle, succeed, try to speak, and immediately discover another invisible wall. In my memory he did eventually speak to the audience – an act which immediately differentiated his work from that of Marceau.

I don't remember hearing of Lecoq's name again until eight or nine years later when I attended another weekend workshop with Buckley in the same room at the same theatre. Lecoq was a mysterious figure for me, someone with whom it was possible to study if you had the money – I didn't.

I developed a stronger interest in Lecoq's work from 1984 when, as a mature student studying for a BA in drama at the University of East Anglia, I was asked to cover the Norwich Mime Festival for the student paper *Phoenix*. Between 1984 and 1989 I covered the Festival for both *Phoenix* and *City Wise*, a local arts magazine and attended workshops and residencies with a host of Lecoq graduates including Théâtre de Complicité, Mark Saunders, I Gelati, Justin Case, John Martin, and Clive Mendus.[2] I also taped interviews with Marcello Magni and Simon McBurney of Complicité, Clive Mendus, and Footsbarn. It was during the interview with McBurney and Magni in February 1984 that I think I first heard the term physical theatre in relation to Lecoq, a term which I was to use but become uncomfortable with in the late 1980s after watching Ben Keaton's *Memoirs of an Irish Taxidermist* (if this is physical theatre, I thought, then what isn't?). I didn't attend Lecoq's master class in 1988 which is a key moment in the formation of the perception of Lecoq-based work in this country. I was, however, applying what I'd learned with a company I'd formed with Dominic Everett in 1986 (Hidden Risk which was later to include sometime Footsbarn members Barry Jones and Mafalda da Camara) in performances and workshops. My work during this period wasn't solely Lecoq based, however, and I drew on a number of other sources and teachers. Any attempt to assess the influence of Lecoq on the British theatre needs to take into account experiences like my own – people who have worked with Lecoq graduates, knowingly or unknowingly, incorporated the exercises, methods, and aesthetics into their own work and then passed them on to others. Such a pattern of influences, which has been growing since 1968 at least, eventually becomes impossible to trace with any certainty back to Lecoq. Perhaps in these cases we should no longer be talking about 'influence', maybe, as Eric Bentley suggested it is a blanket term which 'covers far too large a bed'[3]:

When Jesus appeared in the sky and said, 'Why persecutest thou me?' Saul of Tarsus, a Christian-baiter, became the Christian saint, Paul. That's influence: impact unmistakable and total . . .

Jacques Lecoq: "Tout Bouge" ("Everything Moves"), London International Workshop Centre, Queen Elizabeth Hall, South Bank Centre, 1988. Photo: Coneyl Jay.

Lecoq's 'influence' on the British theatre, if it can be called that, consists not in the adoption of a significant body of theory by critics and practitioners, nor in the visit by a company which exemplifies the 'authentic' Lecoqian theatre in the way in which the visit of the Berliner Ensemble (to London of course) in August 1956 is seen as an 'authentic' exemplar of Brechtian theatre which had a direct influence on subsequent developments within the British Theatre. (Recent visits by Barba's Odin Teatret and The Gardzienice Theatre Association are having an influence in different sections of the British Theatre but, as with the Berliner Ensemble there is a single ensemble connected to a specific guru figure). There is no Lecoq equivalent of Helene Weigel's Mother Courage or Ryszard Cieslak's Constant Prince or Roberta Carreri's Judith. There is no ensemble with whom Lecoq is uniquely associated, no performer who is the Lecoq disciple par excellence. Lecoq offers a method of working, what the students do with it is up to them. He doesn't direct them. He doesn't tell them what to say. Lecoq's school is, as Simon McBurney put it in an interview with me in 1985, 'a school to provoke the imagination; to provoke creativity in the actor so that he is not just another consumable product'. Lecoq's work cannot be 'diluted' or 'polluted' by graduates developing it in their own way, there is no pure Lecoq form and, although there are companies made up solely of Lecoq graduates, graduates are just as likely to find themselves placed with other fringe companies or, given the high profile of Théâtre de Complicité, within the British theatrical mainstream. Whilst Lecoq's influence on individuals may be direct and transformative, the influences of his graduates on the British theatre are more diffuse. Perhaps this explains why Lecoq's name is absent or only briefly alluded to in contemporary studies of British Theatre.[4]

On the other hand, Lecoq's emphasis on provoking the actor's imagination and creativity is a means of freeing actors from the 'tyranny of the text' in order to create their own scenarios. Whilst this is in a tradition of theatrical experimentation and devising which derives from, *inter alia*, Copeau, Stanislavski, Craig, and Artaud most theatre criticism in Britain still focuses on the written text and views devised theatre as somehow inferior. John Elsom in his entry on theatre in the United Kingdom for *The World Encyclopedia of Contemporary Theatre: Europe* (1994) acknowledges that there have been numerous projects which have attempted to do without a writer, but claims that British theatre is still writer-dominated and thus leaves non-text based theatre unexplored. An encyclopedia entry is necessarily restricted in scope and an overview is perhaps not the place for an investigation of the notion of 'authorship'. This question is also left unaddressed by a volume of essays entitled *The Death of the Playwright?* (Ed. Adrian Page 1992) where the notion of the author as individual genius and guarantor of the meanings of a play is subject to investigation but the whole notion of a group of performers devising a piece is left unexplored.

Part of the problem rests with the difficulties in documenting devised performances[5] but there is little difference between a text which has an unwritten physical and vocal score and a piece of dance in these terms.

Interestingly, despite more than forty years of teaching an international clientele, Lecoq is only mentioned in the French entry to the *World Encyclopedia* in the sections on Dance Theatre and training. The latter mention merely mentions the existence of the school in Paris, whereas the former entry describes him as a 'mime' who 'later discovered masks'.[6] This indicates that the problem of assessing Lecoq's work isn't a purely British one.

The emphasis on the importance of literature for the theatre can be seen in the extent to which Théâtre de Complicité have become a force in the British Theatre once they began, firstly to deal with 'classic' playtexts – *The Visit* (1989) *The Winter's Tale* (1992) *The Caucasian Chalk Circle* (1997) – and secondly, to adapt literary classics for the stage – *The Street of Crocodiles* (1993) *Out of a House Walked a Man* (1994–5) *Foe* (1996). Complicité will go down in British Theatre history for these productions rather than the earlier non text-based pieces such as *A Minute Too Late* (1984) or *More Bigger Snacks Now!* (1985). Admittedly the second of these doesn't particularly deserve to be remembered although this, I would suggest, has less to do with the 'inferior' quality of the material and more to do with the overall structure of the piece. But this has to be weighed against the dreariness of *Out of a House Walked a Man* and, particularly, *Foe*, a production which saw the betrayal of (almost) everything that had made Complicité exciting in the past. More recent productions have stayed with staging plays such as *The Caucasian Chalk Circle* (1997) at the Royal National Theatre and Ionesco's *The Chairs* (1998) with mixed results. Leaving aside questions of the aesthetic failure or otherwise of Complicité's recent work, the emphasis on the classics effectively works to keep theatre in its place as a branch of literature.[7] This is ironic when we consider the emphasis which Lecoq places on the body of the performer and the need for each individual to find something to say.

There is, of course, no reason why Lecoq graduates shouldn't work with texts. Being freed from the tyranny of the text is not the same as abandoning the text altogether; if it were then we would be returning to the days of the silent mime. The work of Steven Berkoff is an important example of a Lecoq-derived physical theatre which re-thinks the use of text in a creative way. Berkoff doesn't just add speech to a physical style but reaches for a vocal and linguistic complement. I'm wanting to point out some of the pressures which are placed on companies within the British Theatre to reinforce the importance of text. Perhaps this emphasis on theatre equals text is why dance companies such as DV8, who have picked up the label 'physical theatre' to indicate a break from the traditions of contemporary dance, appear to have fewer problems with the British critical establishment;

Students explore the world of the buffoon under the direction of Jacques Lecoq, London International Workshop Festival, 1988. Photo: Simon Annand.

dancers aren't expected to base their work on pre-existent literary texts. Furthermore, DV8 are more likely to be discussed by dance critics rather than the drama critics who prefer text.

The introduction of DV8 into the debate also draws attention to the work of other companies exploring the boundaries of dance and theatre such as Frantic Assembly and Volcano. This latter company, however, have based their performances on pre-existing texts from Shakespeare's sonnets (*L. O. V. E* (1993)) and *The Communist Manifesto (Manifesto* (1994)) to the plays of Ibsen (*Ibsenities: How to Live* (1994))and Chekhov (*Vagina Dentata* (1996)). The texts in Volcano's productions are exploded and phrases are used as elements in a vocal choreography. The company have not managed to develop their work effectively since *Ibsenities*, however, and the two most recent productions *Under Milk Wood* (1996) and *The Message* (1997) suggest that the company has lost its way. (Interestingly, *Under Milk Wood* fell foul of the Dylan Thomas estate and had to cease touring: a spectral authority exerting textual compliance.) Whilst DV8 was founded in 1986[8] by Lloyd Newson, a former member of Extemporary Dance, and thus has no clear link to the work of Lecoq, the company was formed out of a desire to enable the development of the dancer as a creative artist with something to say. To suggest that there might he a hidden influence from Lecoq on DV8's work would be stretching an idea too far, especially as the emphasis on the dancer having 'something to say' has been an important part of Pina Bausch's work with the Wuppertal Tanztheater since the 1970s. There is, however, a wider cultural connection which owes something to the radical political and social movements of the 1960s and 1970s whilst the linking back to anti-textual developments and to calls for a return to the body in theatrical modernism which hark back to Romantic celebrations of creativity.

Writing in 1908, in 'The Actor and the Übermarionnette' Edward Gordon Craig identified the need for a rigorous physical training of the actor which would include the use of mask, argued that the actor, by virtue of being human would 'revolt against being made a slave or medium for the expression of another's thoughts', and indicated the importance of creativity:

I see a loop-hole by which in time the actors can escape from the bondage they are in. They must create for themselves a new form of acting [...] Today they impersonate and interpret; tomorrow they must represent and interpret; and the third day they must create. By this means style may return."[9]

Whilst Craig recognised the importance of a physical training akin to dance, of developing as a creative rather than as an interpretative artist and thus freeing the actor (and the theatre) from the tyranny of the text, he was taken to task by Jacques Copeau for failing to take on board the responsibility for

Shôn Dale-Jones of Hoi Polloi. Photo © GRM Ward and Reeps.

training such performers.[10] Copeau was, in turn, criticised by Craig for being a 'man of literature' rather than a man of the theatre. Nonetheless, it was Copeau rather than Craig who created a school which focused on the physicality and creativity of the actor and who was to contribute, through his student and son-in-law Jean Dasté, to the early theatre training of Jacques Lecoq.[11] Lecoq himself, however, claims that when he began doing theatre he had 'never heard of Copeau' (see the essay by John Wright in this volume). Nonetheless, it is possible to make numerous direct connections between the work of Lecoq and that of Copeau, not least in the use of the neutral mask as an element in actor training.[12] Whatever links are drawn between Lecoq and earlier figures (Copeau, Artaud, Stanislavski, Meyerhold, Craig) all of whom wrote about developing the creativity of the actor as, indeed, have some more contemporary figures such as Grotowski and Barba, one important difference, alluded to earlier, is that Lecoq doesn't confuse the roles of teacher and director. All of the others mentioned might talk or write about liberating the actor but in the end they keep a directorial control as their teaching was/is a means of furthering their directorial ambitions. Even Philippe Gaulier, a former instructor at the Ecole Jacques Lecoq who has been based in Britain since 1990, gave into temptation and formed the Compagnie Philippe Gaulier. The absence of a Compagnie Jacques Lecoq frees his graduates from both the tranny of the text and the tyranny of the director.

The importance of the conception of the actor as 'creator' is present in all of the contributions to this volume although not all focus explicitly on the practice of improvisation as evidence of such creativity. Entwined with questions of creativity in twentieth-century theatrical discourse are questions about spontaneity and discipline which, for those interested in improvisation, are usually figured by the 'free' creativity of the child and the 'disciplined' creativity of the commedia dell'arte. The dialectical interplay between childhood play and commedia technique is present in all of the articles here, at times marked, but at others remaining a subtextual current.

The emphasis on the actor's body as the starting point rather than a dramatic text is apparent but it is also evident that this shouldn't lead to a narcissistic self-absorption but should always be rooted in an awareness that theatre is *for* an audience (see Murray, Worsley, Mason). David Gaines, founder of Moving Picture Mime Show, hopes to deliver experiences which will (hopefully):

massage every appetite the audience might have, including some they might not have been aware of, and to send them out with a renewed awe and a satisfied glee at the marvelous possibilities of a few people like them, filled with enthusiasm to share an experience or story with the audience, an expectant space, and their own imaginations.[13]

Mark Saunders similarly draws on the image of feeding the audience:

The audience consume [the performance] imaginatively – food for thought, food for their heart, food for their funny bone – whatever it is that needs nourishing. Theatre is, or should give the impression of being, freshly produced each night with fresh ingredients. The actor serves the meal.[14]

Sharing the performance with the audience is a central ethic in Lecoq's teaching and is repeated in different images by a number of graduates. Each performance is a co-creation with performer and audience. Where this complicity is lacking the performance becomes just another convenience product whether it has the name 'Lecoq' stamped on the wrapping or not.

In what follows, Ralph Yarrow picks out key issues arising from the essays in this volume and places Lecoq's work within a wider social and cultural context.

Is there life after Lecoq?

The subsequent essays raise the following main points:

– Lecoq is seen as a *motivator* for actors as authors, placing the emphasis on devising and *co-creation* (initiated in the *autocours* part of his course); the focus of his work is essentially on *form rather than content*, on establishing a method or process of working.
– Lecoq's role is that of a *subversive*, both aesthetically and politically (both explicitly and implicitly he locates his preferred form as an agent for *change*).
– he may he seen as continuing an '*Artaudian*' (physical, anti-verbal) tradition, with perhaps inherent dangers of (deliberate?) one-sidedness.
– he is of major importance as a *mask-teacher* (here the tradition would go back to Copeau).
– he is not a director or writer (except in the sense of revising the import of these terms – there may be parallels here with Roland Barthes' redefinition of those who create meaning from language as *scripteurs*, which includes both production and reception).

Many of these questions are in fact taken up in Frost and Yarrow's *Improvisation in Drama* (Macmillan 1990), which has substantial sections on Lecoq and play, Lecoq as mask-teacher, Lecoq as structuralist etc., and which both contextualises and analyses Lecoq's contribution to the practice of theatre under a number of headings. Most contributors to this volume seem unaware of this material.

The following issues are also implied by or arise from the essays here:

– Does the outreach of his work indicate a kind of Europeanisation of theatrical practice?
– Does the form of much of the work undertaken by his students reflect a Postmodern eclecticism?
– Is there a growth of a 'Lecoq audience', or of Lecoq critics'?
– What is the nature of his 'influence' on established companies, on fringe and touring theatre, on audiences; in drama schools; in University Drama training?
– Can 'physical theatre' be seen as part of a larger move/search, and if so, for what?
– What is his contribution to the emphasis on the semiotics of mime and movement? Do we 'read' him more easily because of it, or does he make it more accessible?
– What is his place in recent theatre pedagogy and what are the similarities and distinctions between Lecoq and other major actor-trainers of the last few decades, e.g. Barba, Brook, Grotowski?

Some responses to these questions would begin to explore for instance the extent to which the kind of theatrical experience offered by Lecoq-trained performers has begun to shift the 'horizon of expectations' of British students, critics, audiences and so on, and/or to map onto the changes which other actor-trainers have set in motion. If such shifts have occurred, they may have profound implications for our understanding of the nature of creative acts, for the empowerment of actors and spectators and for views of the role of theatre in society.

In spite of the fact that this volume deals with Lecoq in Britain, to deal with Lecoq properly requires some awareness of the French context which underpins his work. In terms of practice this may he said to derive in large measure from Copeau (see Frost and Yarrow pp. 20–30); the larger context is that of a focus on the nature of self in (and beyond) language, which would take in Saussure, Symbolist aesthetics, Artaud, Existentialism, Derrida, Lacan and Kristeva at least. Working in Paris means thinking in and/or against this background, which has in Britain often been held at arm's length and regarded as on a par with bizarre ingredients of foreign cuisine. The thing about Lecoq is however that he works with bodies; and that work has to be seen as a challenge to the Cartesian (and Anglo-Saxon) mind-set which separates them from thinking. Lecoq says: "l'homme pense avec tout son corps" (*Théâtre du Geste*, p. 17) and this fundamental position means that when he seeks the initial point of movement he also seeks the impetus of thought and meaning. Here he is on the side of Artaud, but also of Proust and Valéry, Beckett and Sollers. The self that thinks and acts needs firstly to retire from the constructions put upon it by the language of others (through the neutral mask-work) and then to create itself through tactile exploration, observation and discovery, and finally in the company of other similarly questing selves: observation, autocours, presentation. The self is here, as in the work of Kristeva and Cixous, being re-inscribed as performative, within a social and aesthetic context. Lecoq's fundamental notion of the "invention des langages", emerging from and across a "vide", a self-loss and forgetting, exactly parallels the dynamic of Becket's theatre and leads to a 'renovation linguistique' (though Lecoq has a wider sense of 'langue') closely similar to that undertaken by writers of the *Nouveau Roman*, whose aesthetic pushes the reader through a parallel process of defamiliarisation.

If this has indeed 'translated' across the channel, it may be something of a miracle; yet the reception accorded to the work of Lecoq's alumni suggests something of the sort. Not just a 'Europeanisation'; more an intuition, directly transmitted through bodies in space (which is what Lecoq insists form the basic parameters of his work), that theatre can ask the old questions (like Shakespeare): who am "I"?; what is the self?; is it constructed/deconstructed in performance?; how does it present and define itself?; what are its physical/mental roots, impulses, generative energies?; where do "I" stop and "you" begin?

Lecoq-work may produce a form of theatre which is fluid, which reinscribes texts in and through bodies, which reconfigures the experience of being in the theatre. It may also give rise to the sudden shock of recognition, not just of our limitations, but also of the amazement of the ever-present moment when they may be transcended.

Simon Murray adopts Lecoq's own title "Tout Bouge" for his essay; Lecoq himself has said that the improvisatory mode manifests itself most forcefully in periods of major change; Frost and Yarrow highlight Lecoq as one of the most prominent examples of the *improvisatory*, the condition of being ready to innovate. How then has all this working with change resulted in changes in working practices in British theatre? The essays in this volume consider a number of issues in some depth. Lecoq's pedagogy, his use of masks, ways in which individuals and groups have taken on his teaching and his inspiration (and that of Philippe Gaulier) in their work. Other issues are implicit, but are not treated directly, and they need to be prefaced here as a context within which the work of performers and companies occurs.

Fifteen years ago in Britain it was still relatively rare (and exciting) to meet or see or work with performers who had 'done Lecoq'. Théâtre de Complicité, Trestle and Cheek By Jowl were at relatively early stages of their development; Moving Picture Mime Show was the most 'established' ex-Lecoq company, and members of other well-known companies (e.g. Medieval Players, Mummer&Dada) had graduated from Lecoq's school.

Most, if not all, of this work was only visible on the alternative, fringe or small-scale touring circuit.

In the mid 1990s, two main changes are evident. Firstly, some of the companies mentioned above and quite a few performers and directors associated with them have achieved success in more 'mainstream' contexts, though the style of their work is still markedly influenced by their time at Lecoq's school. Théâtre de Complicité is the main case in point. For many years the company was one of the leading exporters of 'British' culture funded by the British Council (somewhat ironic since their ranks, like most Lecoq companies, have always been noticeably Pan-European and much of their work has taken non-British writing as its point of departure). This company, along with e.g. Trestle and Cheek By Jowl, has 'moved up' in terms of economic status and visibility. As a result their work is more generally known to theatre goers and receives regular reviews in the national press (Murray also refers to an interview with Simon McBurney in a BBC tv programme on Complicité).

The second factor is the considerable decline in funding and hence viability of the small-scale touring circuit, due to changes in Arts Council and Regional Arts Board funding. As a result, fewer companies play regularly in such venues, and generally the size of companies and cost of shows has been pared down. There are still old and new ex-Lecoq groups, or groups with a strong Lecoq input, operating (Peepolykus, Brouhaha, Hoipolloi, Bouge-de-là). But the gap between the 'top' and the 'bottom' has become if anything wider and more difficult to cross.

These economic factors have in themselves very little to do with Lecoq's methodology. But in the late 70s and the 80s the relative facility of small-scale funding in the UK tended to create good opportunities for the kind of group which emerged from Lecoq's school – small, close-knit, committed to communal devising and production, temperamentally suited to touring and to responding to the unexpected. Attitudes to employment and the arts in Britain in the 90s are very different. Companies which receive RAB funding now are very likely to be those which are seen as plugging into perceived educational or social needs in specific locations. Almost all touring companies have to include an element of such work in the 'product' they offer. (Many ex-Lecoq companies always did, of course.) So the market is even tougher and the incentive to live permanently 'on the edge' is less obvious.

The questions which might arise in relation to how far Lecoq's work has *promoted* change have then to be seen against a background in which the more immediate economic requirement has been to cope with enforced change. It is however still true that Lecoq's training is an excellent preparation for this: it gives rise to think-on-your-feet theatre which can get up and go anywhere. Indeed, working in such a way and within such an ethos is precisely one way in which Lecoq sees theatre as providing a model not just for coping with but for giving a direction to change.

Concomitantly though, audiences may be more difficult to find in the current climate; and the problem is compounded by economic pressure, in that companies may have less time to 'polish' work. There has always been more than a hint of 'work-in-progress' about much Lecoq-inspired work, and not infrequently this has been developed in performance most successfully. The issue is also in large part stylistic: not that there is a single 'Lecoq' style, as many of the writers in this volume remind us; but there is a way of working which characterises companies and performers. As Bim Mason indicates, it involves a great deal of attention to each aspect of building a move, a sequence, a set of relationships. It is this exquisite and imaginative all-round precision and semiotic richness which has surprised and delighted mainstream audiences and critics in Complicité's and Cheek By Jowl's work, and which is clearly applicable to theatre with or without major reliance on text. But it needs time to develop. In comparison with for instance France and Germany, even the most established British companies have little rehearsal time. There is a real problem here for the continuing availability of work of this quality. On the other hand, in so far as companies like those mentioned have made a major impact (to which should he added that of directors like McBurney, Annabel Arden, Bim Mason, John Martin, Tony Wright, Toby Wilshire), public demand may well ensure that it continues at the top level at least (another example of outreach influence is in successful 'transplants' of companies, directors and performers to e.g. the RSC and the National).

The economics are problematic. But the presence of this kind of attitude to theatre over the last twenty years has begun to change the understanding of the public and the critics. Even, in spite of John Martin's recognisably accurate gloom, in theatre graveyard Britain, new companies are still coming. Audiences, when they can find them, warm to their work. Structural change is taking place: Lecoq's claim for the improvisatory may be tenable.

If it is, by the time we're sure, things will probably have moved on. Now it is rare to meet an actor who hasn't at least *thought* of going to Lecoq, even if finance and lack of French has ruled it out. When anything becomes too predictable, by Lecoq's own standards it's time to move on again. Is there life after Lecoq?

Notes

1. Geoffrey Buckley studied at the École Jacques Lecoq from 1963-66 and specialises in performing Pierrot as the Divine Fool. He is director of the Gelosi

Troupe which aims to present stock commedia dell'arte characters for present-day audiences.

2. It was during two residencies with Mendus at UEA , the second of which resulted in a devised production, that a number of students who were later to go to Paris and study with Lecoq first became acquainted with his work including Shôn Dale-Jones and Jason Turner of Hoi Polloi.

3. Eric Bentley 'The Influence of Brecht' in Kleber & Visser (eds 1990) *Reinterpreting Brecht: His influence on Contemporary Drama and Film*, Cambridge pp. 186-95.

4. John Elsom makes no reference to Lecoq as either a direct or indirect influence on the British Theatre in his contribution to *The World Encyclopedia of Contemporary Theatre: Volume 1: Europe* (Rubin (Ed) 1994) pp.890–934; nor in his *Cold War Theatre* (1992) a study of the British Theatre from 1950–1991. Perhaps this is unsurprising given Elsom's apparent preference for text-based theatre. Lecoq is briefly referred to as an 'influence' on street theatre companies such as Mummer&Dada (see Bim Mason's article below) in Baz Kershaw (1992) *The Politics of Performance* and as an 'influence' on British Feminist Theatre through Annie Griffin and Tattycoram (see Victoria Worsley's article below) in Lizbeth Goodman (1993) *Contemporary Feminist Theatres*. Anthony Frost and Ralph Yarrow (1990) *Improvisation in Drama* is still the only academic text of any significance to pay attention to Lecoq within the context of the British Theatre and Yarrow also acknowledges Lecoq's importance in Yarrow (Ed. 1992) *European Theatre 1960–1990: Cross-cultural Perspectives*. Alison Oddey (1994) *Devising Theatre: A Practical and Theoretical Handbook* makes a brief reference to the 'mime' Lecoq in her discussion of Trestle Theatre (See John Wright's article below). The revised and updated Fourth Edition of James Roose-Evans (1989) *Experimental Theatre* makes no mention of Lecoq nor does Christopher Innes (1993) *Avant Garde Theatre*. Jane Edwardes considers the work of McBurney and Arden with Complicité in her 'Directors: The New Generation' in Theodore Shank (Ed. 1994) *Contemporary British Theatre* with a passing reference to LeCoq (sic), Gaulier and Pagnieux (sic). The situation is different, however, in terms of actor-training see, for example: Anne Dennis (1995) *The Articulate Body: The Physical Training of the Actor*, John Martin (1989) *The Mysore Manual*, Lea Logie 'Developing a Physical Vocabulary for the Contemporary Actor' *NTQ* Vol. XI no.43 August 1995 pp.230–240 and Nesta Jones 'Towards a Study of the English Acting Tradition' *NTQ* Vol. XII No.45 February 1996 pp.6–20. Most information on Lecoq in the UK can be found amongst the pages of various issues of *Total Theatre*.

5. An investigation of this difficulty was the subject of several events organised by the Centre for Performance Research, Cardiff (now Aberystwyth) in 1993 and 1994. See also *Contemporary Theatre* Review Vol. 2 Part 2 *British Live Art: Essays and Documentations*, 1994 (Issue Editor: Nick Kaye).

6. Philippe Rouyer in *The World Encyclopedia of Contemporary Theatre: Europe* p. 309.

7. Some of the problems of wanting to see theatre as being both textual and separate from literature are examined in Benjamin Bennett (1990) *Theater as a*

Problem: Modern Drama and its Place in Literature. For Bennett 'drama' is inescapably a 'literary type'

8. This is the date the company was officially founded although the first production, *Bein' A Part, Lonely Art,* was devised and performed during 1985. For a critical history of DV8 see Fiona Buckland 'Towards a Language of the Stage: the Work of DV8 Physical Theatre' in *New Theatre Quarterly* Vol. XI, No.44, November 1995, pp.371–380, also Ana Sanchez-Colberg's 'Altered States and Subliminal Spaces: Charting the Road towards a Physical Theatre' in *Performance Research* 1(2) Summer 1996 pp.40–56. There is a significant absence of Lecoq in Sanchez-Colberg's account the path of which is determined by its end focus on dance-based physical theatre.

9. Craig (1980) *On the Art of The Theatre,* Heinemann Educational Books p.61.

10. Rudlin, John and Norman H. Paul (Ed. and Trans. 1980) *Copeau: Texts on Theatre,* Routledge p.22.

11. Leabhart (1989) *Modern and Postmodern Mime* and Frost and Yarrow (1990) discuss the relationship of Lecoq's work to that of Copeau.

12. For a study of the Neutral Mask see Eldredge, Sears A. and Huston, Hollis W. (1978) 'Actor Training in the Neutral Mask', *The Drama Review*, Winter 1978 pp. 19–28, reprinted in Zarrilli (Ed. 1995) *Acting (Re)-Considered*, Routledge pp. 121–8. See also Frost and Yarrow op. cit. 63–71; Yarrow, Ralph (1986) 'Neutral Consciousness in the Experience of Theatre', *Mosaic* XIX/3 pp.1–14.

13. E-mail to the editors August 1996.

14. Letter to the editors August 1996.

2

"TOUT BOUGE"[1]: JACQUES LECOQ, MODERN MIME AND THE ZERO BODY. A PEDAGOGY FOR THE CREATIVE ACTOR.

Simon Murray

Mime becomes popular in a transitional period when theatre is in decline and is moving towards renewal. Theatre needs a heightened sense of movement because when the spoken word cannot express itself fully, it returns to the language of the body.[2]

The words of Jacques Lecoq, quoted here when teaching a master class in London for the 1988 International Workshop Festival, provide a useful frame for a period where – in the view of the director of London's Royal Court Theatre, Stephen Daldry – there has been "an explosion of form in British theatre".[3] The extent to which this *explosion of form* has permeated all levels of British theatre is debatable, but the features which characterise such an eruption can be identified. At risk of oversimplification these may be summarised as a revolt against the all-pervading psychological realism exemplified by the theatre mainstream; a concern for the visual dimensions of theatre production; a refocussing on the actor/performer's body as a source of messages and meanings on stage; the performer as a co-creator of equal significance to the writer and director in the production process; attempts to find a satisfactory interrogation between movement and spoken text; and finally a concern with both *play* and ritual as the process and product of creating work.

Compared to other key figures who have influenced the shape and direction of theatre in the second half of the twentieth century – Brook, Barba, Grotowski, Beckett for example – little has been written about Jacques Lecoq. He is a teacher, but one whose pedagogy is constantly refreshed and invigorated by a commitment to research both within and outside his Paris school. However, apart from time spent in Italy between 1948 and 1956, Lecoq has rarely directed work for the public theatre and thus there are none of the more tangible reference points which might have illustrated a distinctive or unique approach to dramaturgy and mise en scene. Instead, any attempt to describe the actual consequences of his pedagogy for the stage has to be conducted at the remove of unravelling his influence through the process and product of those theatre practitioners who once trained with him.

In the *UK Mime and Physical Theatre Training Directory* (1993)[4] out of 66 entries in the section entitled *Practitioners and Performing Companies*, 17 acknowledged Lecoq as a significant influence in their own approach to training and education. A further 17 entries listed Philippe Gaulier and/or Monika Pagneux as 'indicators' of their teaching style. Whilst Gaulier and Pagneux have clearly forged their own unique pedagogy, both were senior teachers at Lecoq's school until they left to form their own establishment in 1981 and thus may be perceived as teaching from within broadly the same canon. Hence, over 50% of the practitioners identified in this directory who currently teach in the field of physical theatre derive influence from Lecoq (or from two of his ex-teachers) in the way they interpret their educational work. Although such statistics are crude and reveal little of the quality and precise direction of the teaching offered, they serve as a useful measure of Lecoq's impact in the field of physical theatre training in this country. By comparison, Etienne Decroux and Marcel Marceau receive few references in the Directory. To establish the contrast is not to pass judgement on the respective merits of these figures and the theatre aesthetics they espouse, rather it is to suggest that the statistics offer a revealing, if rough and ready sociological indicator of Lecoq's influence in this country, if not in others.

As has been suggested above, an aesthetic which sites both the visual dimensions of performance and the actor's body and its movement is one of the defining features of the *explosion of form* identified by Stephen Daldry. It is in these areas that the influence of Lecoq may be detected. The tag of 'physical' is increasingly attached both to the skills required of actors in job specifications and as a descriptive label for theatre companies as they promote and try to encapsulate their style of work. No longer is this confined to small scale product on the experimental fringe, although it is in this sector that such phraseology still seems to be most prevalent. That so diverse a range of publicly funded companies such as Red Shift, Théâtre de Complicité, Trestle, DV8, Paines Plough, the David Glass Ensemble, Forced Entertainment, Black Mime Theatre and Volcano amongst many other lesser known groups, have regularly chosen to invoke the *physical theatre* label (or some variation on the same) is a matter of significance, but also a source of some confusion. Whilst at the broadest level it is indicative of a cultural shift in the way a number of important practitioners choose to construct their work and – as importantly – describe it; the choice of terminology also reveals – given the disparate nature of both the process and the product of such companies – just how difficult it is to identity what a *physical theatre* actually is.

It is not the purpose of this essay to investigate these issues, but it is clear that a number of different technical traditions feed into and shape what is popularly described as physical or visual theatre. The influence of Lecoq in this historical and cultural pantheon is evidently significant but must be considered alongside other traditions such as dance, live art, the circus and music hall, the conventions of Eastern dance theatre, the corporeal mime of Decroux and the work of the theorist/practitioners such as Grotowski and Barba.

Drawing upon the experiences of three Lecoq trained performers, I will attempt to explore four key features of his pedagogy and consider the significance of these for the style of theatre perceived to be representative of practitioners who have studied at Lecoq's School. The only detailed account in English of Lecoq's teaching is to be found in Mira Felner's book, the *Apostles of Silence*, published in 1985. Thomas Leabhart's *Modern and Post-Modern Mime* (1989) contains a chapter on Lecoq and, whilst more discursive, covers similar ground. Lecoq himself has edited and contributed chapters to a book entitled *Le Théâtre du Geste* (1987), but to date this has only been published in French. In an attempt to reach beyond a crude reformulation based simply on chapters in the Felner and Leabhart books, I sought to discover further information from Alan Fairbairn, Beatrice Pemberton and Jon Potter who were interviewed between December 1993 and January 1994. All three trained at Lecoq's school in the mid to late 1980's and are thus now 6 or 7 years into their performing careers.

Interviews and Methodology

The interviews were qualitive in methodology and wide-ranging in the ground they covered, but all three were asked the same questions. Although possessing no first-hand knowledge of Lecoq's teaching, my own training in Paris for a year (1986–87) with Philippe Gaulier and Monika Pagneux, occasional visits to his school during this period to watch student performances and subsequent 'consumption' (as spectator) of the work of many Lecoq trained theatre companies, had provided me with a relatively strong – if impressionistic – sense of Lecoq's style and aesthetics. To this picture – and a thorough reading of the Felner and Leabhart accounts – the interviews sought not only to add detail, but also to construct 'profiles' of three Lecoq trained artists who were well into their careers and who had followed, out of a mixture of choice and circumstance, differing paths.

The questions posed to the respondents were divided into three areas: their background and motivations for going to Lecoq; their actual experience of the school; and their subsequent working life as professional performers. The second area of interest attempted not only to elicit factual information on the 'how' and 'what' of the school's pedagogy but also to uncover their feelings and sense impressions at the actual time of the experience, and not with the wisdom of hindsight. The third bank of questions offered an opportunity for each of them to reflect on how the skills, beliefs and practices they had acquired during their time with Lecoq had been modified or reinforced by subsequent experience.

Information gleaned from these interviews provides neither an exhaustive account of the form and content of Lecoq's teaching, nor does it offer the definitive profile of the *Lecoq student* and a stereotypical performing career which ensues. A sample of three self-evidently cannot achieve this but, more importantly, any attempt to fix and set in concrete Lecoq's 'method' would be to deny the developing and incremental nature of a pedagogy which is constantly refreshed by research and a quest for new ideas. Nonetheless, the interviews not unexpectedly revealed certain patterns of response from the three artists as well as interesting areas of contradiction and paradox.

In conversation, the performers sometimes used the term 'Lecoq companies' as a way of situating the work of theatre groups, some or all of whose members had once trained with Lecoq. I have continued to use the phrase as a convenient shorthand, but am well aware of how reductive it must sound. To describe, for example, Théâtre de Complicité as a 'Lecoq company' would be to deny both the range of influences which inform its work and the creative self-development which all members of that Ensemble must have undergone over the last 12 years. To a greater or less extent this applies to any company, no matter how much a Lecoq pedigree is invoked in programmes or publicity statements. Nonetheless, the prevalence of ex-Lecoq students working together in companies, and their sense of a need to share a 'common vocabulary' is significant and has to be acknowledged as such. The issue also highlights the difficulty facing any commentator when attempting to assess Lecoq's influence on contemporary theatre.

Performer Profiles: Background and Motivation

Alan Fairbairn was at Lecoq's School between 1985 and 1987. With a degree in English and Drama, an MA and a teacher's certificate, he had been working at a VIth form college in Manchester before committing himself to a professional career in theatre.

After taking a degree in Philosophy at Newcastle University and a teacher's certificate, Beatrice Pemberton had spent nearly three years working in an experimental theatre company she helped to set up with three ex-university friends. She enrolled at Lecoq's School a year later than Alan and spent two years in Paris between 1986 and 1988.

Jon Potter entered the Lecoq School in 1986 and thus often worked alongside Beatrice for the two-year duration of the course. Unlike the other two, Jon came straight from a degree in English and Drama at Manchester

Alan Fairbairn (left) and Gordon Wilson of The Primitives in *Cook It*. Photo courtesy of The Primitives.

University, but had performed in many student productions and at the Edinburgh Festival.

Unsurprisingly, the three performers had similar perceptions as to what the Lecoq school might offer, but each placed a different emphasis upon what seemed most important. Both Beatrice and Alan were removing themselves from a career pattern they found unsatisfactory at the time: for the former it was an 'escape' from a particular approach to making theatre, the latter from institutionalised teaching. An empathy with the qualities of 'essentialism and economy', an interest in Beckett and the clown and a pleasurable re-evaluation of mime – as both concept and practice – were, for Alan, the defining factors which led him to Lecoq. For Beatrice, the anticipation of acquiring a 'physical performance vocabulary' and an approach to making theatre which embraced less 'thinking and talking' seemed to be the most important elements she hoped to find at the Paris School. For Jon, the continued opportunity to devise and create his own work, and the prospect of a stimulating internationalism at the school, were the driving forces behind the decision.

It is significant that none of the three performers identified the school as an institution which taught *acting* as such, but for all – consciously or implicitly – enrolment at Lecoq signified an escape from the 'dominance of text' in English theatre. Finally, it is an affirmation of Théâtre de Complicité's impact, even in the mid 1980's, that all three cited this company – amongst others – as influential in their decision to study with Lecoq.

Lecoq's School: Organisation, Curriculum and Selection

The interviews did not attempt to elicit an exhaustive or descriptive account of the school's weekly or monthly curriculum over two years. Given a degree of existing knowledge about Lecoq and his pedagogy, I made a conscious selection of those areas which I wished to prioritise. From time to time the interviewees' own priorities properly diverted the discussion down unanticipated paths, and these in their turn revealed new issues which before I had not considered. In order to place the central features of Lecoq's teaching in some kind of context it seems important initially to offer a summary account of the School's structure and organisation.

The School's structure is inevitably a function of Lecoq's own teaching priorities and the issues which come to the fore through his ongoing commitment to research and intellectual exploration. Consequently, the curriculum may change slightly from year to year. Within these possibilities of flux there are clearly many constants in Lecoq's approach which appear to stand the test of time, and best exemplify what his training has offered to thousands of students over a period of nearly 40 years.

The School's publicity announces that the course will last for two years, that the first term is a "trial period during which both the School and the pupils decide whether the pupil is to continue or not"[5] and that there is a third optional year devoted to pedagogy. In a typical year approximately 100 students are accepted on the submission of a cv and a teacher's reference on the aspirant's ability in movement. At this stage selection does not appear to be particularly systematic, as Alan wryly points out:

I don't believe there was any selection – except the size of your cheque book.

Nonetheless, a rigorous process of selection does exist at the end of the first year and – to a lesser extent – after completion of the initial term. Although it is largely through their own choice that students leave after one term, entry into the second year is a very different matter, and all three respondents spoke with animation about the nerve-racking process they had gone through at this juncture. Whilst typically between 5–10 pupils will leave after the first term, entrants for the second year have been whittled down to about 35.

The fees for the School are considerable: in 1987 they were 18,000 francs a year – i.e 6000 francs (approximately £600) a term. Since then, according to Alan, these have been raised by about 10% every year. Regardless of any concept of 'value for money', the sums must be substantial for both prospective and actual students, and – as with any system of fee-paying education – have sociological consequences for the social class background of the majority of pupils.

Classes run from October to June, take up 5 half days a week and are taught by a team of 5 or 6 teachers working alongside Lecoq. All teachers must have been students at the School and completed the third optional year in pedagogy. In Alan's year, students would have as a minimum, one class each in movement and improvisation with Lecoq himself, amounting in total to between 3 and 4 hours a week contact time. For Jon and Beatrice there was more time with Lecoq due to the absence of another teacher. A further optional possibility for students – and one requiring additional payment – is attendance at Lecoq's own series of evening workshops known as the LEM (Laboratoire d'Etude du Mouvement). This is a forum for the articulation of Lecoq's research and continuing investigation into the nature of all movement. Within the structure of LEM[6] lectures are also given by an architect with whom Lecoq has worked closely for many years. At the end of the year LEM students make a presentation at the School of their 'research'. This may take the form of three-dimensional installations and models and/or performed movement pieces. Only Jon of the three performers elected to follow the LEM while in Paris, but all three attested to its importance as an arena for Lecoq's research.

Lecoq's Pedagogy: The Role of Mime, Neutral Mask, Autocours and Play

Using material from the interviews and drawing upon the accounts of both Felner and Leabhart, the following sections will attempt to paint a picture of what lies at the heart of Lecoq's pedagogy. A comprehensive analysis of every element of Lecoq's teaching is well beyond the scope of this article, and – to a certain extent – has been achieved by Felner in *The Apostles of Silence*. Here, inevitably, significant areas of the curriculum such as commedia dell'arte, chorus, the search for one's clown, expressive and larval masks and *bouffon* theatre are not considered.

Mime and movement.

The spinal column of the School is the analysis of movement. Analysis of movement is not necessarily the analysis of the body, it is the analysis of all movements, even of animals, of plants, of the dynamics of passion, of colours, of everything that moves.[7]

Directly beneath the logo on a 1980's prospectus for the School is the phrase *Mime and Movement Theatre*, thus encapsulating in three words the main thrust of Lecoq's pedagogy. Amongst contemporary practitioners and critics mime rates highly in terminological demonology, often being rejected for the more all-embracing, if tautological, *physical* – or *movement* – theatre. If for Lecoq the two are almost synonymous it is because of the pains he takes to render explicit the difference between the *mime de fond* (fundamental or essential mime) and the *mime de forme* (mannered, virtuosic mime or pantomime). Students' exploration – collectively and individually – of the *mime de fond* lies at the heart of their experience of the School, and is the bed-rock upon which their skills and qualities as performers must be constructed.

    That *explosion of form*, claimed as a characteristic feature of contemporary British theatre by Stephen Daldry, is foreshadowed by one side of another Lecoq binary: the *mime du début* versus the *mime de la fin*. The latter occurs at the end of an era in theatre when form is well defined; the former when theatre is seeking redefinition and new meanings. Clearly, Lecoq's school aims to nurture the *mime du début* amongst its students. Felner offers a comprehensive account of the way in which Lecoq uses these terms, but further insight into his approach to movement can be found in a publication which outlines the curriculum to prospective students. It is a school of 'dramatic creation' and one that is directed towards a 'theatre and a mime that is renewed and broadened by each creator.'[8] A corollary of this is Lecoq's antipathy towards both the actor as *interpreter* or as an instrument for the display of (someone else's) *technique*, and the codification of mime into a rigid aesthetic which locks shut the performer's potential for creativity.

With the British I have to strip down their interpretive training. Mine is a school of creativity. I remind the actors that they are 'auteurs'. The task is not to interpret: you must re-live each phase physically.[9]

From his opposition to the 'performer as interpreter' model of acting, *and* the codification of mime, it would seem that Lecoq is at odds with both the 'psycho-techniques' which have dominated professional theatre training in the West for much of this century, and with the *grammaire*[10] of Decroux. An example which well illustrates Lecoq's views on the relationship between performer, movement and technique, is revealed in an exercise known as the '20 Movements' which students have to do in their first year. Alan explains:

You have to put twenty Decroux-based movements into some kind of order of your own choosing and (then) perform them in front of the whole school. Quite intimidating. My memory is that you are led to believe that this must be technically rather good and that those who are (technically) better will have more chance of getting into the second year. However, this is not true at all, because the great thing about Lecoq is that he is interested in what you might call 'theatrical presence' rather than technical aptitude.

Jon slightly modifies Alan's interpretation of the exercise:

Lecoq concentrates on the technique of doing them accurately and will pull you up at the end if you've done them wrong – or if you have only done nineteen. On the other hand what is interesting for him – and the audience – is *you*. Even with a fixed undulation of the body, down to the smallest movement of the wrist – you see right through to the person underneath. You see all kinds of personal rhythms and ties. Some people are very funny and they don't know why and that's always very interesting to observe.

This apparent contradiction between the necessity of technical correctness and the importance of 'theatrical presence' is highlighted by Beatrice and Alan:

To be quite honest I thought that the *20 Movements* was an incredibly tedious exercise, especially when you are told that 'pure technique' is boring. The actual process ...... didn't interest me , but once it starts fitting together you see the point. Lecoq is always interested in the 'purity' ...... in the truth of the movement. (BP)

Often the people who had more impact were less good technically. They did the exercises very comically and caused a lot of laughter – unintentionally because everyone was trying to do it seriously. They were much more impressive as performers. The technical dimension is there to give you more assurance in movement ..... it certainly isn't the *raison d'être* of the School. In Lecoq's case, the most important thing for him in theatre is that the actor should attain on stage – in whatever style he is performing – something which he would call 'truth'. (AF)

The performers' comments on the *20 Movements* illustrate that whilst Lecoq is happy to 'borrow' a technical exercise from Decroux, it is as the means to an end, rather than the objective in itself which is significant. A neutral and disciplined execution of the movements is required, but only as a framework to reveal what, in fact, is most interesting: the presence and truthful 'purity' of the performer which lies beneath. Alan recollects one student who had worked for the circus and who was a skilful acrobat:

He could do all the technical exercises perfectly, but to watch him do the *20 Movements* was remarkable because he seemed to diminish when he was doing them. He had absolutely no presence whatsoever.

It is interesting to compare the performers' use of the term 'presence' with its centrality to the work and thinking of Eugenio Barba, director of Denmark's Odin Teatret. Both in his writing and practice, Barba constantly addresses the issue of 'presence' in a performer.[11] For him the achievement of 'presence' is based on the quest for a state of 'pre-expressivity', a condition whereby the performer is no longer in the daily idiom of (physical) existence but not yet in an 'expressive' mode. Training for 'pre-expressivity' is rare in Western theatre, but fundamental to the forms of Oriental dance dramas. For Barba, 'presence' is predicated upon the performer's mastery of the principles of 'pre-expressivity'. The relationship between Lecoq and Barba's approach to theatrical presence deserves further investigation, but is beyond the scope of this article.

Analysis of movement, the body's potential for creative expression, gestural 'honesty', and a fluidity and economy of movement: all are themes which run across the curriculum throughout the two years. Specific skills may be acquired in sessions devoted to acrobatics, juggling, *pantomime blanche*[12] and in Commedia dell'Arte, but even in these one has a sense that any particular expertise acquired is almost incidental to the wider purpose of equipping students with a level of corporeal confidence and that physical *openness* upon which the elusive quality of 'presence' is predicated. In the 1970's, Monika Pagneux was Lecoq's senior teacher of movement awareness and her approach, based upon the pioneering work of Moshe Feldenkrais and epitomised by the phrase, 'liberating the body', has – to a certain extent – been continued by other teachers in the years which followed her departure from the School in 1981.

In the first year, however, students are invited to forget all the enculturated habits of socialized movement and to make a 'simple journey'[13] which will last for many months. The discoveries which are made during this period ultimately determine the students' 'success' in dealing with the specific theatrical styles taught in the second year. This *cleansing*, or forgetting process, is inextricably bound up with Lecoq's use of the neutral mask – perhaps the most significant tool in his array of teaching techniques. It also leads directly to the core of Lecoq's philosophy and to what differentiates his work from that of Decroux.

Returning to zero and the neutral mask

In the beginning , it is necessary to demystify all that we know in order to put ourselves in a state of non-knowing , a state of openness and availability for the rediscovery of the elemental. For now, we no longer see what surrounds us.[14]

This is the challenge which Lecoq proposes to his students at the beginning of the first term and with which they will have to wrestle throughout the year. Jon recalls Lecoq's opening words:

We begin at zero and we are going to make a very simple voyage.

To understand the reasons which lie behind this process of demystification, we are led to the – controversial – centre of Lecoq's philosophy of mime and human movement. Felner offers a summary of his analysis in three terse, but revealing phrases:

Gesture precedes knowledge. Gesture precedes thought. Gesture precedes language.

Even such a précis of the hypotheses which underpin Lecoq's approach, suggests a position with which whole sections of anthropological and cultural theory might take issue. For Lecoq, thought occurs after movement. He is thus inviting his students to explore a "primitive form of symbolizing"[15] which is untainted both by language and a motivation born out of either intellectual reasoning or emotional need. It is this pattern of non-socialised movement and gesture which Lecoq calls the *mime de fond*. While it is beyond the reach of this article to investigate Lecoq's analysis in relation to anthropology or linguistics, it is worth noting that his theoretical position signposts certain connections – and oppositions – with other major figures of 20th-century theatre. Although extreme caution is needed in making comparisons which may only be tenuous and superficial, that Lecoq assigns significance to the 'primitive' in his teaching would seem to align him with other key names in European avant-garde theatre. Artaud, Jarry,

Barrault, Grotowski, Barba and Brook, for example, have all – at different times – explored and experimented with notions of the 'primitive' in their work.[16] Moreover, Lecoq shares with these figures a commitment to a physical, non-naturalistic theatre language which stands in opposition to psychological realism. The extent to which Lecoq himself would happily locate himself within such a tradition is unclear. In searching for an asocial, acultural gestural language (*mime de fond*) Lecoq implicitly would seem to assign a universal and timeless quality to 'primitive' movement. However, Lecoq is primarily a teacher and someone whose reputation is linked not to theatre productions he has directed or scripts he has written, but to a school. There is little evidence that he advocates a spiritual celebration of the 'primitive' as source material for the productions created by his students, past or present. Nor indeed do the many Lecoq trained performers and companies (working in Britain) seem unduly concerned with such subject matter. The process of 'returning to zero' and subsequent use of the neutral mask may perhaps be seen as little different in practice from the concern of many theatre teachers that their students should discard the tics, mannerisms and other physical or linguistic over-elaborations which they assume contribute positively to their craft.

Finally, before the performers' responses to the neutral mask are considered, it is worth noting where Lecoq stands in comparison to Decroux over the relationship between movement, thought and language. In *Paroles sur le Mime*[17] Decroux writes:

Everything is permitted in art, provided it is done on purpose. And since in our art (mime), the body of man is the basic material, the body must imitate thought.

The dichotomy between the two men is thus exposed: for Lecoq, as we have seen, the body (and its movement) *produce thought* and hence the student of theatre must strive for the 'natural' gesture which is uncorrupted by socialized intention, while for Decroux it is *purpose* which determines movement – the body, in other words, *translates* thought.

At the School the 'stripping away' process – tackled largely through the neutral mask – dominates the first year. Lecoq takes his students through a series of exercises, many of which are based upon those developed by Jacques Copeau and Suzanne Bing at the Vieux Colombier in the 1920's.[18] Under the mask, students progress through a number of incremental stages – identification with the elements, with matter, with animals, with colours – culminating in exercises where characterisation is permitted. At certain points the mask is removed but students are expected to sustain the same 'purity' of gesture or movement throughout. Within the process, students must find the inner rhythm of the material they are exploring and the respiration appropriate not only to the quality of the matter itself but also to the dynamic of the group,

The three performers have positive memories of the value of the neutral mask, but all found the 'stripping away' process a difficult and testing challenge. Beatrice describes an exercise:

Waking up for the first time – how do you wake up? You have no experience; there's nothing behind; there's no fear, no feeling; no anger. How does a mask get up? You had to go over and over this. There's so much in your head which you don't realise is there. The neutral mask was brilliant – the ultimate in purity. All completely new to me.

Because of her particular theatre background the experience was perhaps more than usually tough:

You don't ask questions and you don't get answers. You learn through *doing* and your body is supposed to absorb it all. It's an anti-thought process – no words. Even having to improvise without talking about it first was totally new to me. At the beginning I was often accused of being too 'scolaire' and intellectual.

For Jon the problems were similar:

You must learn an economy of movement. I was having to deal with things which 4 years of university acting had given me .... a fair amount of arrogance I suppose. (At the beginning) I was caught because they were asking for economy, sincerity, involvement – to avoid tricks and not to try too hard – but at the same time when I did try things which to me were sincere, they were very boring!

Alan affirms the value of the neutral mask and stresses its timeless qualities as a learning device:

It's a tool of amazing, quite incredible power. When people put it on and perform often you see them have no impact whatsoever because their face is covered up. It's quite hard to work out why some people suffer from this stage deadness with the mask on. It's to do with élan, energy, timing, sensibility of fooling etc.

The neutral mask is never something you learn to do – it always remains a tool whereby you try to improve on your previous performances and explore new things. I think its something I could usefully do again in 5 years time.

Autocours

The autocours – students working in groups without teachers on a given theme to be performed at the end of every week – is a key element in the School's curriculum, and consumes no less than one and a half hours of each working day. Simon McBurney, Théâtre de Complicité's director and co-founder, interviewed in a recent publication entitled *Food for the Soul* traces the origins of autocours to the student rebellions of 1968:

Even the pupils in his school were affected by '68 .... they turned over the whole school and refused to work. They said to Lecoq, we don't want to work, we want to teach ourselves. And Lecoq, who's the constant responder and observer, said: every day for an hour you will teach yourselves. And it was called autocours.[19]

Perhaps more than any other single feature, the autocours gives Lecoq's institution its identity as a "school of creativity" rather than as a place where students are taught 'acting' or 'drama'. Through the autocours students are offered the opportunity to express their voices as *auteurs*, and it is here that Lecoq's rejection of the 'actor as instrument' is most manifest.

For Jon, as we have seen, the chance to be involved in the "whole process of theatre" – to devise and make his own work – was a significant factor in determining the decision to study with Lecoq. Alan, however, was slightly shocked by the prominence given to autocours:

Initially, I felt a bit cheated that a third of the School's working day was given over to an untaught activity, but, of course, performing every week in front of other people is what you do in theatre life. It [autocours] was Lecoq's invention and few teachers would have had the audacity to send students off unsupervised for 90 minutes. I later came to realise that this was one of the most important aspects of the School.

The process confronts students with all the problems of group dynamics, the difficulties of communication across different languages, the challenge of working quickly and effectively, and the sometimes painful consequences of competitiveness and exclusion. This latter point is well articulated by Beatrice:

The competitiveness means you are always thinking 'who do I work best with'. In the autocours there are really tight groups – you almost form 'companies' and exclude others from working with you. The same people do the work over and over again, leaving those who have not bonded – or who have not got that kind of conviction – in 'weak' groups.

The experience of autocours often breeds consequences beyond the School itself. If you are lucky or strong enough, the process of forging a creative bond with others of a similar interest and rapport may lead to the formation of an embryonic company whose life is established at the end of the two years. This was the case for both Jon (Talking Pictures) and Alan (Théâtre Décalé). Beatrice, too, after working with other groups, joined Watson and Co, a company formed by another ex-Lecoq student.

Craig Weston (left), Gordon Wilson and Alan Fairbairn (The Primitives) in *Cook It*. Photo courtesy of the Primitives.

At its most effective the autocours clearly nurtures a range of qualities which students can carry with them into their professional careers. Skill at devising, alacrity and imagination in producing material, a spirit of constructive cooperation and an openness for 'play' are often features – at least for a time – of 'Lecoq companies', and whose lineage can be traced back to the experience of autocours. However, despite all its positive features, the three interviewees allude to a sense of unease felt at the time and/or in retrospect. Jon hints at the issue which is framed succinctly by Beatrice and stated at its most unequivocal by Alan:

In the bars afterwards we would constantly discuss: 'why are we doing this ......
what are we trying to mean'. Even at that early stage we were aware that Lecoq
was not interested in this kind of question. Lecoq would give you the means of
saying things, but couldn't be involved in what you were saying. He'd respond to
what he saw and say whether it was effective or not. It was up to you to take
responsibility for what you were saying. As far as he was concerned everyone has
something to say. (JP)

The autocours teaches you how to make a piece, but not about what you are saying
in this piece. (BP)

It is certainly something which has led to the kind of work we now see from Lecoq
trained performers. I think the Lecoq set-up breeds the fallacy that everyone has
the potential to be a 'writer'. The truth of the matter is that every actor has the
potential to make an individual contribution to a show. (AF)

The points made here raise in their turn a whole range of further questions about form and content, the role and dispensability of writer and director and the broader politics of Lecoq's School. In relation to the issue of form and content it is interesting to note that, on the comparatively rare occasions when drama critics from the national press review physical or movement theatre, this is often an area they pick up on. *The Guardian*'s Michael Billington, for example, has been fulsome in his praise for Théâtre de Complicité's recent productions, but admits:

In the first 8 years of their existence Complicité established their brilliant and
dazzling acrobatic and mimetic skill, but they have also bred in me - and I think
some others as well – a kind of counter reaction which is whether the moral content
of theatre is being subordinated to a display of technique .... it was sometimes a
feeling that technique was actually overlaying content.[20]

Whether Billington is right or wrong in his judgement on the earlier work of Complicité, or whether theatre critics, habituated to text based drama, have an adequate understanding of the 'language' of a physical theatre (and a critical vocabulary to match) is a pertinent and debatable issue. The point of interest here, however, is the degree of similarity – superficially at least – between the views expressed by *The Guardian's* theatre critic and the reflective and questioning observations articulated by the three Lecoq trained performers themselves. These issues are considered in more detail in the final section.

Play

The idea and practice of *play* is one of the most important qualities in Lecoq's pedagogical framework, but also one of the most elusive to define. Neither Felner nor Leabhart mention the term in their accounts, but as an approach to making theatre, and in the practice of performing it, *play* is one of the most characteristic properties to be observed in the work of those companies who acknowledge a debt to Lecoq. In the choice of a name for their company, the founder members of Théâtre de Complicité clearly wished to highlight one quality of the work they were going to bring to the public's attention in the early 1980's. Complicité – the English equivalent (complicity) fails to capture the spirit of the French – suggests an alive, vibrant and engaged rapport between performers, and performers and audience. It is, in a sense, an *outcome of play*.

Unlike Philippe Gaulier who runs an entire course entitled *Le Jeu*, Lecoq does not seem to confront *play* head on. Alan, however, is in no doubt as to its importance:

The whole notion of *play* is essential to Lecoq's School. The most important element of *play* .... always seemed to be connected with making the most of whatever material was available theatrically when you were on stage at any particular moment. I think *play* is about rendering the moment on stage into life – bringing it alive – exploiting the moment.

Beatrice stresses another dimension to *play*, namely its communicative quality:

It's about the quality of interaction between you and the audience and your fellow performers. Yes, it's a difficult idea and Lecoq does not actually teach it. I think Lecoq teaches you how to make a simple idea work, but not how to make a simple idea develop.

In a different context, teacher and theatre director, John Wright, neatly encapsulates the notion of play by giving an example of how Philippe Gaulier injects the idea into a scene by suggesting some additional business – "exploiting the moment" (cf Alan above) – and thus breathing life into a situation which was hitherto dead:

"Just kiss each other on the nose between the words", he (Gaulier) said to me as I creaked through a scene from *Romeo and Juliet*. Suddenly our mood lightened, we laughed, and the text took on new life.[21]

Play is therefore a dynamic principle which informs the quality of interaction between performers and with their audience, but also opens up possibilities for action which can both liberate the actor from the 'literalness' of the text and enrich it with additional (physical and visual) meaning.

It is important to note that although *play* is often associated with a performing style which has been influenced by the teaching of Lecoq and Gaulier, it is not confined to them. Tim Etchells, director and writer with experimental theatre company Forced Entertainment, offers a perceptive account of what the idea means to him and his colleagues:

It is an attempt to shift the boundaries of real time and real space. *Play* is looser than games – it has a chameleon-like, immutable quality. It allows a shift of rules, a shift between different positions – an 'I can change the paradigm we are working in' quality. If you ditch psychological narrative it's easy to lose sense of anything happening. *Play* (and competition) are useful in making dynamic what would otherwise be a purely presentational image.[22]

Although in many respects the work of Forced Entertainment is far removed from a style of theatre we perceive – rightly or wrongly – to typify those companies nurtured by Lecoq and Gaulier, there is a clear correspondence between Etchell's words and those of Alan Fairbairn quoted above.

In conclusion, we can locate Lecoq's notion of *play* as part of that wider terrain which offers the actor the opportunity to express his/her voice as *auteur* and not simply as a mouthpiece and interpreter. On the one hand, *play* is that light and alive quality which all theatrical interaction should ideally possess, and, on the other, it is the imaginative space claimed by the performer to create material beyond the prescription of both director and the written text. This freedom to embrace the mantle of *auteur* carries with it, for the actor, risks as well as opportunities. In such a context, Beatrice's earlier observation that Lecoq teaches students how to make a simple idea work, but not how to make it *develop*, is relevant. Alan echoes Beatrice's feelings and indicates that *play* is also potentially hazardous territory for the actor:

If you've done Lecoq, you can probably devise a quite funny and interesting five minutes around how to make a cup of tea, whereas another writer might pass over that as an unimportant incident. Of course, that may become something wonderful, surreal and dreamlike, but there might be some questions posed at the end about the value of the writing. It will always be a problem in theatre of what you are saying and why you are saying it.

The Practitioner as Art-form and the Problem of Writing

The conversations with Beatrice, Jon and Alan provided a stimulating insight into the 'Lecoq experience', often revealing a positive consensus on many aspects of the School. However, their responses also unveiled a number of difficulties – or paradoxes – with which, as professional theatre practitioners, they were often wrestling. These issues – some of which are explored below – signpost the need for a more comprehensive analysis of Lecoq's pedagogy, and its consequences for performance, than is possible within the scope of this piece of writing.

Beyond all the specifics of Lecoq's School there appears an ever-present belief that it is the body and the imagination of the actor which lie at the heart of any dynamic and vibrant theatre. The stripping away of habituated conventions (both mental and physical), a rejection of codification with a consequent antipathy towards technical virtuosity, and the constant encouragement given to the students' creative capacities are central both to the practice of the School and Lecoq's own ideological make-up. Implicit in this paradigm is the assumption that it is the actor's imagination which creates theatre as much as the writer or the director. The autocours as a pedagogical device, and *play* as a critical quality in the actor's armoury and mind-set, are further means to achieving this objective. In an interview with Lecoq in 1988, theatre writer and critic, Jim Hiley, summarises the essence of his approach and the style of work we often see from performers who studied at the School:

Lecoq and his followers' successes have made the most eloquent case yet for the practitioner as art form, and the abandonment of make-believe.[23]

Although the career patterns of the three interviewees have, of course, been different in their particular details, it is significant that a feature common to all of them has been a commitment to making *devised* work. While Alan and Beatrice have worked with various companies, none of the three opted to become 'jobbing actors' in the sense one normally understands the term. One imagines – at least in the early stages of their careers – that such a strategy is typical of many ex-Lecoq students. The devising process takes many forms and this is evidenced by the performers' accounts of the work they have made since leaving the School. In describing various productions, all three regularly alluded to varying degrees of difficulty and anguish over lines of demarcation, authority and responsibility in the performer/director/writer relationship. Clearly such difficulties are potentially present in any devising process and are not peculiar to – or simply provoked by – actors with a Lecoq training. The point, however, is whether, in Alan's words,

Rob Gardner (left) and Jon Potter of Company Paradiso, 1997–8. Photo courtesy of Company Paradiso.

"the Lecoq set-up breeds the fallacy that everyone has the potential to be a writer". Several months after leaving the School, Alan established a company in Paris with two other Lecoq-trained performers. He describes the episode:

We worked for about 10 months on a show which brought to light all the problems of working in a Lecoq style. As a group we had a strong resistance to having a director. It was very democratic which I now think is extremely hard – impossible, if everyone has an equal say, if nobody has a final veto, and no-one has enough vision to see globally where the whole thing is going.

Subsequently, as a reaction to the problems they were having, the group worked with several writers and directors and finally after only a few performances the piece was abandoned: "the tensions were so great ...... we either had to separate or explode." Alan observes that it was "quite a salutary experience ...... the kind of thing many Lecoq-trained students go through." This, and subsequent experiences, have convinced him that:

If you put together three actors from Lecoq it does not mean that a good piece of writing is going to come out of it. Some kind of mechanism has to exist - this could be a writer, a director or a strong personality.

Talking Pictures, the company which Jon helped to establish with other Lecoq performers from his year, has always worked with outside directors, the majority of whom have not had a Lecoq training. He explains the Company's philosophy:

We do think that as a group of actors it's important that we share a sense of Lecoq – a language of performing. In a sense we have relied on directors to be the writer – the *auteur* – of the piece. We feel it's better to work with a close knit group of actors and so give the director a sound base.

Jon notes how their pattern of devising has changed over time:

At the beginning we used to spend more time on our own because we thought it was very important to have control over our own material. We would make it (the material) and then present it to the director. Now we find it important to have the director there from the beginning, but to have time by ourselves during the process to make material.

However, even though Jon states that the Company's relationships with their directors have been constructive and amicable, there is a sense from his account that they still have not found the perfect 'chemistry':

In our last show we used Sandra – a teacher from Lecoq – as our director in order to go back to where we came from – to try to develop our own aesthetic a bit more clearly – because we felt that each of these (previous) shows was heavily influenced by a director. We were feeling a bit like a performance company without any line in terms of our own theatre aesthetic. I think that we had a line in terms of preoccupations and areas of subject matter, but not in style.

Beatrice, however, whilst acknowledging many positive aspects of the School's pedagogy, does not share that sense – most strongly articulated by Jon – of the need to work alongside other Lecoq trained actors. She admits:

I don't feel I'm a Lecoq person really. Just because you've trained at the same place is not in itself a reason for wanting to work with someone. It does not automatically mean you have a common vocabulary.

Her career pattern reflects this sentiment and only when working with Watson and Co on a couple of productions has she performed with other Lecoq actors. In her interview Beatrice often revealed an unease about what she defines as the typical Lecoq style of performing. In contrast to Jon and Alan she seems to have distanced herself from a number of the axioms normally associated with the School's approach.

At the end of their time at the School Lecoq tells students that it will probably take them at least five years to assimilate everything they have experienced, and that the two main areas not covered during the course are writing and music. By 'writing' we must understand him to refer to the broad issues of composition and dramaturgy and not simply the skills entailed in the creative act of playwriting. It is this lacuna in the curriculum – candidly acknowledged by Lecoq – which often seems to be the focus of external criticism levelled at the style of work associated with 'Lecoq companies'.

It is arguable that this issue is not simply a consequence of any formal absence of dramaturgy and composition within the School's curriculum, but is also intricately bound up with what Jim Hiley suggests is a key characteristic of Lecoq's aesthetic, namely the concept (and practice) of "the practitioner as art-form". Beyond the confidence nurtured by autocours and the imaginative skills foregrounded by emphasis on *play*, the question relates to the wider politics of Lecoq's School of 'dramatic creation'. It is to this issue which the final section of the essay now turns.

A Politics of the Imagination

At the end of each of the interviews the performers were asked whether there was any identifiable politics (in the broadest sense) to Lecoq's teaching and to summarise what they felt was axiomatic to the School's culture and precepts. All three interviewees agreed that there was no explicit political 'line' running through Lecoq's pedagogy, and Beatrice speaks for the others when she says that "he is not interested in giving a message – not interested in personal ideology at all. In terms of politics it's quite apolitical". Alan agrees, but also suggests a sub-text:

Since he keeps a distance from his students – and that's an admirable thing – you never really get to know what his political views are, or indeed his views on anything. There's no political mission, though I think at a profounder level people are encouraged to be subversive. The whole Lecoq style subverts, if you like, conventional theatre practice. People are encouraged to be very individualistic.

The spirit of individualism runs through much of Lecoq's own writing with its regular emphasis on the importance of liberating the actor from preconceived notions of the world and in his rejection of systems and 'ready made' aesthetics. This disposition is put in context when one examines what Lecoq appears to be looking for in the individual performer. Beyond the difficult and opaque notion of truthfulness which Jon, Alan and Beatrice often cited as a quality Lecoq seeks in his students' performances, the importance of having something to say occurs regularly in their accounts. Jon explains what Lecoq means by this term:

You are good when you find this *quelque chose à dire* (something to say). It's a phrase he uses which I think is very interesting, because coming from my background I had always connected *having something to say* with being political. But Lecoq's *quelque chose à dire* is a very personal thing. When you are communicating something effective about your world – or yourself then you are finding something to say. Everyone has something to say.

Beatrice links the quest for truthfulness with this *quelque chose à dire*:

What Lecoq likes is when he sees people being honest and using whatever it is that they are good at. If that happens then it works as a piece of theatre.

Thus the idea of "practitioner as art-form", which at first reading may have appeared to connect with the typical practices of live Art – the denial of conventional theatrical representation and so on – now appears as something rather different. If Jon and Beatrice's comments reflect a correct understanding of Lecoq's position, then *performer as art form* seems more to do with a personal quest of self-discovery, the outcome of which – in performance terms – is the individual or collective expression of a voice. If this happens then the piece 'works' as theatre. The concept can be further narrowed by suggesting that *having something to say* is largely achieved by sensate means – through movement and physicality – rather than as a consequence of cerebration.

Lecoq's suspicion of an approach to making work which is overly intellectual or theoretical and his pleasure in finding performers with *something to say* is made clear by Jon who affirms:

There's a rejection of things which are esoteric or 'arty' very, very much. He says 'would my sister understand this' as a kind of criteria for how clear a piece is. Pieces must work for a general audience. All these styles – commedia, melodrama, clowns – they are popular forms aren't they?

Lecoq's delight in popular forms of theatre and his concern that pieces should work for 'general' audiences seems to be reflected in the productions one often associates with companies influenced by a Lecoq training. Alan recalls a conversation with René Basinet whom Lecoq esteemed as the best mime artist in Europe: "He once said to me that what you learn at Lecoq is how to be commercial. I think this has a lot of truth in it."

Certainly the success and popularity of companies like Théâtre de Complicité, the Right Size and (in the 1980's) the Moving Picture Mime Show have helped to shift public perceptions away from the notion that modern mime or physical theatre must inevitably be esoteric, incomprehensible and elitist. Similarly, the numerous clown performers working on the streets of Europe, whose style has been directly influenced by Lecoq's teaching methods, attest to his interest in popular forms and in the use of comedy and humour as a vehicle for having *something to say*. Perhaps as a rider to these observations, it is interesting to note how rarely does one read of 'Lecoq companies' being invited to perform in some of Britain's more self consciously experimental venues such as London's Institute of Contemporary Arts (ICA), Manchester's Green Room or Glasgow's Centre for Contemporary Arts (previously the 3rd Eye Centre).

At this point a question can be raised as to whether there are any limits to Lecoq's encouragement of 'creative freedom' and his invocation that the regime must liberate himself from 'systems and ready-made aesthetics'. Whilst the point was not explored in great detail in the interviews, a difference between Jon and Alan surfaced over this issue. When invited to summarise what they found most valuable in the Lecoq experience, part of Alan's response was to say:

One of the great things about the School is that everything is permissible – its postmodern quality – providing it is alive and true in some way. Lecoq would probably laugh if you said he was an example of postmodernism, but my definition of it is having the right to mix different disciplines together.

Jon offers a different interpretation on this question, directing his answer towards the issue of representation on stage:

No, I don't think everything was permissible. Of course there are many different styles you go through and a huge range of different relationships you have with an audience, but they are all 'up-front'. No-one ever investigates that area of whether you are *performing* or not. That territory – which I was very interested in before I went to the School – is not explored. For Lecoq, if you are not *performing* he stops it. He would only allow things to happen in front of the curtain – those pieces where people present their work and walk off again. There is no notion of who is performing and who is not, or of challenging the stage space.

Although Beatrice did not refer directly to this issue one senses from her other comments that she would probably have aligned herself to Jon's position as to whether everything was 'permissible'. Had the two performers been face to face, the contrast between Jon and Alan's views might have been explained by a confusion over frames of reference. Nonetheless, Alan's response chimes with Leabhart's evaluation when making a comparison between Decroux and Lecoq:

Lecoq's teaching has been a perfect antidote to Decroux's; if either one had not existed, he would have to have been created .... Decroux is a pure modernist .... Lecoq is already something of a postmodernist in that he foresaw the synthesis that was to come and has in fact encouraged it.[24]

Lecoq's own statement in a brochure describing the School is relevant to this debate. He proposes that the ultimate aim of his training is:

To liberate mime from the sclerosis of formalisms, creating the fundamentals of a dramatic formation completely based on the body, pitting the student face to face with himself in a state of perpetual discovery.[25]

His withering rejection of the "sclerosis of formalisms" and emphasis on "perpetual discovery" suggests – at first sight – that Lecoq has an ambiguous relationship with the conventions of Modernism. His interest in the 'play' of different forms, in the rejection of codification and a certain flexibility and pragmatism in the making of theatre do provide hints of a more postmodern identity. However, with his stress on 'individuality', in his quest for a 'rediscovery of the elemental' and through all the essentialist implications entailed in 'beginning at zero' and of 'movement before thought' Lecoq seems to fit more into a modernist/humanist aesthetic than a postmodern one. It seems that if the debate is framed by the conventions of twentieth-century mime then certainly there is a pluralistic – if not exactly postmodern – quality to Lecoq's thought and practice. However, if the net is thrown wider to encompass the huge range of forms represented in contemporary experimental theatre there are indeed definable limits to what he believes is 'permissible'.

Conclusion

Any attempt to construct a comprehensive framework in which to evaluate Lecoq's contribution to contemporary theatre runs up against the difficulty of how exactly to assess his influence. If contemporary academic theatre criticism and semiotic analysis warns us off any attempt to understand a piece of theatre merely by attributing 'authorship' to either writer or director, how do we begin to place the contribution of the teacher?

That Lecoq has 'confined' himself to teaching, research and running a school for 40 years means – as has been stated before – any rigorous attempt to trace his influence into the actual product we may see on stage from those companies whose members once trained with him, must inevitably be a tortuous business. While such a project runs the risk of being absurdly reductivist and of doing a great disservice to both Lecoq himself and the companies studied, sensitively undertaken it is perhaps the only way to arrive at a sophisticated evaluation of his influence.

In the meantime we have only his own writing, a limited number of accounts from other authors and the testaments of students past and present. Some selected comments from the three interviewees provide a warm, if eclectic, summation of the main precepts they have taken with them from Lecoq's School.

Anti-intellectual and anti-acting. He places a huge importance on humility within the actor. Images are based in a truthful physicality. Simplicity – reducing an idea to its simplest form in order to understand it, and then to develop it. (Beatrice Pemberton)

How to operate effectively on stage so that you are saying things that are important to you and the other performers involved. The sense of internationalism – a belief that we can make theatre together between peoples. (Jon Potter)

Actor's theatre rather than director's theatre. A degree of assurance on stage – you can feel this élan when you are performing – it all comes out of this notion of play which is so central to the School's teaching. The School is very alive – there's a great deal of vigour and energy there. The pedagogical approach is always developing. .... always evolving. (Alan Fairbairn)

Apparently Lecoq often protests that he is simply "a man who wants to go back to his home and feed his chickens". (JP) In his 1988 *Observer* interview with Jim Hiley there is an appropriately self-effacing comment from Lecoq, containing both the essence of his philosophy and a fitting horticultural analogy. He says:

I don't want my pupils to love me. Good and evil don't exist in teaching, nor do prescriptions, only analysis of how things move. I'm like a gardener who knows how to make a carrot grow better than others. But I could never turn it into a turnip.[26]

Postscript

The interviews upon which this essay is based were conducted in 1994, and the piece itself was written in the same year. Inevitably, certain aspects of the analysis might have a different shade if the article had been written more recently. The three performers interviewed – Jon, Alan and Beatrice – are still creators of movement theatre, although the contexts in which they work may have changed since they were first interviewed.

Notes and References

Thanks to Alan Fairbairn, Jon Potter and Beatrice Pemberton for their cooperation in the interviews and to Nigel Stewart (Lancaster University) for his constructive comments as the essay was being written.

1. "Tout Bouge" (everything moves): the title of a lecture demonstration given by Lecoq.
2. Lecoq, quoted in *Guardian* interview with John Vidal. Tues 22nd March 1988.
3. Stephen Daldry, currently artistic director of the Royal Court Theatre in London, quoted in interview with Giles Croft (September 1992.) Published by the Royal National Theatre in *Platform Papers*.
4. *UK Mime and Physical Theatre Training Directory*, 1993. Commissioned and published by Mime Action Group (MAG).
5. Extract from a prospectus for the Lecoq School, mid 1980's.
6. In *Modern and Post-Modern Mime* (Macmillan 1989) Thomas Leabhart writes "An undated flyer for the Laboratoire (LEM) lists the following areas of study as part of its programme: sensitizing of the body to space; analysis of movement; the dynamism of forms and colours, an organic approach to words; sound transfers; the drama of constructed spaces; playing of passions; states and situations; gauge of the body; dynamic objects; spatial structures of the body; portable architecture; animation; masquodrome; video; projects."
7. Lecoq, quoted in Leabhart from an unpublished interview with Francis McLean, April 1980.
8. Extract from a prospectus for the Lecoq School, mid 1980's.
9. Lecoq quoted in interview with Jim Hiley, *The Observer*, Sunday 20th March 1988.

10. Decroux's *grammaire*, established with Jean-Louis Barrault, was a strict and comprehensive codification of movement and gesture which would enable mime to attain the status and authority of an autonomous art-form.
11. *The Secret Art of the Performer*, Eugenio Barba and Nicola Savarese, (Routledge 1991).
12. *Pantomime blanche*: 19th century form made famous by the French mime, Jean-Gaspard Debureau. *Pantomime blanche* drew on commedia dell'arte, but made the character of Pierrot the focal point of the action.
13. From Lecoq's opening remarks to a group of students in 1986.
14. Lecoq, quoted in Mira Felner's book *Apostles of Silence* (Fairleigh Dickinson, Associated University Presses, 1985) from "L'Ecole Jacques Lecoq", *Théâtre de la Ville*, no 15, January 1972.
15. From *An Introduction to Anthropology* by Beals and Hoijer (New York, Macmillan, 1964) quoted by Felner.
16. *Avant-Garde Theatre 1892–1992*, Christopher Innes, (Routledge 1993).
17. Etienne Decroux, *Paroles sur le Mime*, (Paris: Gallimard, 1963).
18. The company of the Vieux-Colombier was established in 1913 by Jacques Copeau as a theatre laboratory whose main purpose was to revitalize French theatre through research, training and production. Actress Suzanne Bing was one of Copeau's senior teachers at Vieux-Colombier specialising in movement.
19. Simon McBurney, Théâtre de Complicité, quoted in *Live 1. Food for the Soul* in an interview with David Tushingham, (Methuen 1994).
20. Michael Billington, theatre critic on *The Guardian*, quoted from the 'Late Show' (BBC Two) which profiled Théâtre de Complicité in rehearsal for *The Street of Crocodiles*, August 1992.
21. Theatre director and teacher, John Wright in a profile of Philippe Gaulier, *The Stage* (1991).
22. Tim Etchells, director and writer with Forced Entertainment Theatre Cooperative, quoted from a lecture given during Sheffield course, April 1993.
23. Lecoq quoted in Hiley interview, *The Observer*, Sunday 20th March 1988.
24. Leabhart, *Modern and Post-Modern Mime*.
25. Lecoq quoted in Felner, from *L'Ecole Jacques Lecoq*, brochure.
26. Lecoq quoted in Hiley interview, *The Observer*, Sunday 20th March 1988.

3

THE WELL OF POSSIBILITIES: THEORETICAL AND PRACTICAL USES OF LECOQ'S TEACHING

Bim Mason

This article describes the way in which aspects of Lecoq's teaching have influenced my work over the last ten years. Some of these aspects are fundamental to all the work, others have been springboards for ideas in specific areas of work. It is my intention to attempt to summarise the entire teaching but merely present a personal account of what has been useful. However, because I am assuming that not all readers will be familiar with the precise nature of Lecoq's teaching, I have considered it necessary to include some explanation of these aspects before going on to show how they have fed in to my work. This work covers a broad range of small-scale touring work including physical theatre, circus theatre, street theatre and mask theatre in the roles of performer, director/devisor, teacher and mask-maker. Because Lecoq's teaching is so broad-based it has been invaluable in all these areas.

The first thing to say is the most obvious. Lecoq's approach to theatre (and other art forms) is by means of the body. He does not exclude the spoken word or deny its importance but he is concerned to reinstate the body as the basic means of communication. His is a theatre of action and physical image rather than an interplay of ideas and concepts. So, for example, the short time devoted to text was not about interpretation but about the physical and vocal rhythms within it. He takes a tough line on 'psychological' acting. He promotes a human drama where the protagonists are pushed and pulled by passions so strong that they take extra-ordinary action; the source of human drama is therefore visceral rather than cerebral.

For my work within the field of street theatre this is the ideal approach. In the streets it is difficult for an audience to listen to large amounts of speech because of the problem of surrounding noise, so visual image and action are a much more effective means of communication. Street theatre and literary theatre are not compatible. Circus too is primarily a physical and visual medium, although with the addition of music, lighting and the enhanced focus, a greater sense of mood can be created. For both these areas and, of course, for all physically based theatre it is essential that the body is finely tuned to convey the appropriate quality. I have found that the use of the neutral mask and the study of movement qualities has been indispensable in helping all kinds of students become aware of their characteristic physical habits and limitations.

Lecoq was always stressing the word 'efficace' meaning both efficient and effective. In terms of movement the less there is the more effective it can become. Gesture, like music, can be a better means of communication than words. For example a light touch on the cheek will probably be more effective than saying 'I love you'. Moreover the effect is not doubled by adding the words; it is inefficient and less effective. In this sense the work should be a series of Zen strokes – clear, accurate and simple, aiming always to capture the essence of the subject matter. This approach not only applies to movement but also to devising. I have found it to be most important to avoid the tendency to add ideas onto other ideas, embellishing it to the point where it becomes like a structure whose essential form is hidden under a mass of ornamentation. It is satisfying to build up layers of meaning in order to give a rich texture to a piece but one must beware of cluttering to the point where the initial idea becomes obscured.

Lecoq's approach is analytical but the analysis is always firmly rooted in actuality – phenomena that can be observed, studied and referred back to. At the end of the first year the students are given the task of studying an 'ambience' – a place with an atmosphere – and, by studying the rhythms and qualities of movement within it, to represent it, not in a naturalistic or narrative way, but by means of physical image and action. Observation of real life is common practice in drama schools but Lecoq also uses a much broader range of source material – natural phenomena of every sort, colours, qualities of lights, of music, different materials, atmospheres and even architecture. Phenomena that, of course, need to be treated in order to be interpreted by the human body. Recently I have become aware how important it is to locate a show in a specific environment, not only to colour the background of a drama but also so that the environment can reflect the inner state of the protagonists. For example the Peepolykus show, *No Man's Land*, that we created in early 1994, is set among urban garden allotments; a semi-abstract sequence portraying nocturnal predators reinforces the atmosphere of suspicion and acquisitiveness between the allotment holders.

The construction of movement sequences was perhaps the most fundamental part of the Lecoq training. I had been acting for several years before experiencing Lecoq's teaching and it was a revelation to realise that any piece of movement could be analysed, broken down into its constituent parts, ordered, clarified, re-constructed and given a new life. This was the recurring theme at the school, whether it was a work action, a movement from sport, a piece of *pantomime blanche* or an extended sequence from a Chaplin film. Having to learn a sequence of up to a hundred and twenty separate movements with their correct rhythm, tension and breathing patterns gave an infinite variety of possibilities to explore. For physical comedy this method is why sometimes you get a laugh and why sometimes you do not.

Recently I was playing in Pinter's *The Caretaker* with Kaboodle at the Liverpool Everyman. Within a short run it was impossible to fully explore all the nuances of action within the piece – how many steps into the room before stopping, of what size and rhythm, what is the breathing pattern? How extended, tense, long is that arm gesture? This continuing research keeps the performances alive during a long run when more conventionally trained actors may feel they have arrived at doing it the best way they can much sooner and therefore lose the freshness of playing. Of course, a director may be able to give detailed physical instruction but unless the actor is used to working in this way they will not be able to remember long sequences and they tend to resist working in such a technical way.

This method made it possible to create movement sequences when using mime. My first solo show, *When You Gotta Go*, used mime to create the room in which the piece was set. At one point it was necessary to erect an ironing board. It would seem a simple operation but is in fact quite complicated and not surprisingly it is not one of the stock mime sequences that are taught. I used a real ironing board to see what the operation involved and then re-created the sequence adding nuances of gesture because I had learnt from Lecoq that although one uses real life movements as the raw material, they have to be accentuated in order to clarify the meaning of the movement for the public.

There are two dangers with constructing physical routines; firstly that they remain as displays of technique – the dramatic action is only a pretext for the routine and the acting loses quality while performing the routine. Secondly that the acting takes over to the extent where the technique becomes inaccurate. With some skills this can become dangerous – a good example of this is in the teaching of stage fighting. Using the Lecoq method I encourage students to break down the action – preparation moves, action, appropriate reaction, extending the body, timing, impulses and so on, building up a sequence purely technically without acting. The moment they are instructed to add in the acting by means of vocal sound they find it hard to resist the excitement and they revert to the playground; accuracy is lost and this not only spoils the effect but can lead to accidents. Thus in constructing all routines the balance between focus on technique and emotional acting has to be carefully maintained.

Working as I do in both theatre based work and work based on circus skills this balance is a constant issue. The actors tend to find it hard to master technique because they are used to working in a way where their physical actions are the result of physical emotions and these may slightly differ each time. They find technique too artificial, lifeless and constricting. The circus performers, on the other hand, find it harder to give actions much feeling because they are used to working from the exterior actions using constant repetition through practice. They find the whole business of acting unpredictable, indefinable and frustrating, devoid of learnable systems. Because Lecoq's teaching works both from the inside to the outside (in the improvisation classes) and also from the outside to the inside (in the physical technique training), it provides a whole range of tactics to deal with this crucial issue.

In the Mummer&Dada outdoor shows we tried to strike a balance between tight physical routines and sections that were open for improvisation. The routines, usually acrobatic, slapstick, or musical numbers but occasionally centred on magic and juggling, could not easily be interrupted. The precision of timing and the high level technique gave the whole piece a hard-edged dynamism and discipline to balance the looser, free improvisation. It also gave us a secure foundation so that if audience and the surroundings did not give us much to improvise on then we had the routines to rely on. It was this combination of improvisation and routines that had particularly interested me when we studied Commedia dell'Arte at the school. Having played Harlequino himself, Lecoq has a great love of the Commedia but he encouraged us to reinvent it and not, as many groups have tried to do in the past, make a historical reconstruction. To do this would, in any case, be self-defeating as the purpose of the Commedia dell'Arte was to get away from the scholarly approach that had tried to recreate the long dead theatre of the Classical era.

One of the characteristics of Lecoq's work that sets it apart from all other drama training, including Philippe Gaulier's, is the emphasis on abstract work. Most drama training focuses on the actor playing human characters usually within a figurative, if not naturalistic context. Lecoq bridges the gap between theatre and the world of dance, in that the human body is used to express not only the figurative world of animal, mineral and vegetable but also the abstract world of colours, music and emotions. Specific movements are identified for each. It is different from the world of dance in that, for example, when moving to music it is not a question of using the music as accompaniment but instead moving in order to **be** the music.

Whilst at the school I attended the twice weekly evening classes which formed the Laboratoire d'Etude du Mouvement. These explored the relationships of colours, space and emotions, using the same criteria as was used for analyzing movement – weight, size, rhythm, dynamics (push/pull) and tension levels. I was fascinated by an exercise in which we examined the effect of different spaces as we journeyed from one end of the school to the other and then translated this experience of the architecture into movement. We also made manipulatable objects that could be moved in a way that corresponded to the construction (e.g. tense moves with sudden stops correspond with straight lines and sharp corners). This created an extraordinary effect which brought the inanimate objects to life.

This work connected with my Art School training and was invaluable for stenography, costume, lighting and publicity design. More importantly it gave a whole new direction for my mask construction work. Most mask-making tuition in Britain focuses on either the techniques of different materials or on stock character types, be that Commedia, Archetypal or otherwise. My focus over the last ten years has been to construct masks that could not only 'come alive' (by appearing to change expression) but which also proposed specific movements in the way that the manipulatable objects, described above, had done. I am continually looking for ways to explore and develop this highly specialised area. The abstract work has made it possible to collaborate with those from a visual art background such as Welfare State and with choreographers such as Helen Crocker. It has also enabled me to appreciate and be influenced by Live Art practitioners such as IOU and physical theatre groups such as DV8 in their concern for mood and atmosphere. These influences have fed directly into scenes for *No Man's Land*, mentioned above, and given to that show another dimension to the clown narrative.

Whilst it is true that some of this abstract work can only be fully appreciated by those with an eye for movement, Lecoq continually stressed that the aim is always to communicate to the spectators. If the spectators do not understand what you are doing then the object has been defeated. This may seem obvious but it distances him from the strands in British theatre work which are more exclusive, either because the meaning would only be clear to a sophisticated audience or because the work is of a ritualistic nature in which the full significance of the actions needs to be understood by the performers but not necessarily by the spectators, as is the case in some Live Art.

One of the aspects of Lecoq's teaching that I have found most useful is the whole subject of the relationship with the audience. He always stresses the importance of playing 'for' the audience and not turning the piece in on itself. However, going further in this direction, he also deals with the performer making direct contact with the public and this, of course, is essential for outdoor performance as well as some indoor styles. Audience relationship is not dealt with as a subject in itself but different types of relationship are utilised while studying the subjects of Storytelling, Oratory and in the Clown and Bouffon styles.

A particular exercise that opened up many possibilities was that in which two storytellers take it in turns to tell us a story, occasionally disagreeing about what was supposed to have happened. These disagreements could become arguments so that in effect it is like watching two actors at a rehearsal disagreeing over what the script should be – the audience therefore witnesses the 'offstage' relationship of the actors. Although there was no direct audience contact, a similar sense of a play within a play was explored when we were studying the Clown style and were asked to devise a piece about a clown rehearsal, similar to the Mechanicals' scenes in *A Midsummer Night's Dream* except that it could be a rehearsal for a film. This 'alienation technique' is familiar to British audiences through television comedy – Morecambe and Wise and Monty Python. It is an ideal format for telling a story in an outdoor environment where it is essential to be able to respond to unexpected and intrusive phenomena such as dogs, drunks, police and rain.

The Mummer&Dada street shows worked without a set. They were done three-quarters in the round with only a box, drum, banner and perhaps a costume rail at the back so that 'backstage' jobs such as changing costume were done in full view of the public. Because the actors could step in and out of role at any time it was possible to improvise outside the roles but within the piece. This gave several layers to the performance. The actors introduced themselves one by one saying where they were from (six different nationalities). This was done using what I call stage personas – not exactly how we are in real life but close to it – we exaggerated certain true aspects. For example, in *Hell Is Not So Hot* I played a benevolent, slightly pretentious, ineffectual dictator-director. It was therefore possible for our real-life selves to comment and make fun of each others' on stage persona. At the next level there was the character role we were playing. These roles were appropriate to each persona in the way that appears to happen with amateur dramatic companies – one will always contrive to have a magnificent costume, another will always end up with the uncomfortable, ignominious parts. As pretentious director I, of course, played God. Our whip-cracking, knife-throwing French anarchist played the Devil. Our ridiculously multi-talented young American (magic, acrobatics, trumpet & juggling) played the intrepid, romantic hero. As mentioned earlier these characters were sometimes disguised which gave a further level of play within play. These four levels made it possible for us to comment on the action as it was going along although great care had to be taken to play fully when in role and not to parody. Given the frequency and ease of dropping in and out of role it felt comfortable to the audience when we responded to the unpredictable – when there were moments of audience participation, either on or offstage, we were able to communicate person to person as well as character to person. Similarly we could deal with an intrusion into the playing area without embarrassment or a drop in the action.

From a director's point of view probably one of the most important contributions Lecoq has made to British theatre is his encouragement to mix styles. He was chiefly responsible for the heresy of mixing mime with the spoken word. At the school he is constantly experimenting with mixing mime with storytelling and melodrama or with mixing melodrama with tragedy. He is excited by the idea of using the chorus outside the context of classical tragedy. He has embraced Postmodernism and rejected the purism of Marceau. In this mixture there is, he recognises, the danger of a 'soup', in which the constituent elements lose their value, so he is very clear about the potential and function of each style. For him the five styles of Tragedy, Melodrama, Clown, Bouffon and the Commedia dell'Arte are the fundamental reference points for all theatre.

Nowadays in British theatre we see much of this conscious mix of styles – John Wright's Tragic Clown, The Right Size's Clown Buffoon, Complicité and Talking Pictures' mix of storytelling, melodrama and mime images. Mixing of styles is a constant fascination for me. There seem to be two ways to mix them within one piece – by integration or by juxtaposition. In the first case the problem is how to integrate the skill and routine while avoiding the kind of awkward and unconvincing transition that happens, for example, in musicals where the shift is from naturalistic acting into song. This can be a big problem in circus theatre, in fact it is *the* problem.

This problem is tackled at Lecoq's school while studying Melodrama. Students are encouraged to find a way to use songs as a means of conveying more emotional impact than otherwise possible. This might, for example, be the remembering of a song from childhood sparked off by seeing a long forgotten object or it might be a rousing chorus associated with a work action or a sense of homeland. There are many different tactics to find a smooth transition in and out of 'the number' but it is essential to avoid a drop in the level of acting whilst engaged in the technical routine. This is not easy if the routine is difficult or dangerous, inappropriate facial expression is the most obvious manifestation but we may also see preparation moves or even a complete reversal of the dramatic action such as the cooperative cueing signals at the beginning of a juggling fight. Audiences for the Mummer&Dada shows found it refreshingly different that we did not present and bow at the end of difficult routines but continued with the dramatic action. (We might briefly acknowledge applause if possible but would never cue it.)

Juxtaposition of contrasted styles can be very effective. We discovered this in the second Mummer&Dada show where after a clownish knockabout acrobatic fight the hero is killed and we suddenly switched into tragedy with a gutsy, solo, Flamenco lament. This shocked the audience. I developed this idea of juxtaposition in my most recent solo show, *Fallen Arches*. The aim was to surprise the audience with switches of style after every scene, almost in the way that an evening of cabaret might contain many different types of acts; thus there were different kinds of dance routines, a mime routine, a clown routine, a stand-up comedy routine, a mask and puppet routine and a routine using animated contraptions. This was all loosely linked around the subject of feet, with a vague, absurd story and themes about self-image and conditioned ideas of aesthetics. The switch of styles meant that constant play could be made with the fourth wall. The experiment was not to integrate the styles in any way but to juxtapose them in order to prevent the public from settling into the kind of easy classification that always occurs within the first few minutes of a play.

In *No Man's Land* we used both integration and juxtaposition. It involved half-masked eccentric clown characters in a melodramatic story about territorial conflict between gardeners. Within this story there is a buffoon parody of the situation in former Yugoslavia. There are integrated sequences using live music, mask and puppet, mime, magic, animated objects and circus skills (for example a character does a back somersault as an expression of joy). Juxtaposed with this story are semi-abstract images based on plant, animal and insect movements, partly using larval/Basel-type masks. We used mime when we were interested in the choreography of digging movements and a real spade when the manipulated object proposes a clown routine. This is all anathema to the purists but for modern audiences it works very well. The interspersal of such a rich mix of material requires short scenes and smooth transitions. However, this rich mix can be appreciated on many levels, from sophisticated audiences to children and takes a step in the direction of creating the kind of universal theatre which has been my interest.

Of all the theatrical styles that are covered at Lecoq's one that is least well known in Britain is that of 'Bouffon' – the buffoons, those who are rejected by society and create their own hierarchy, making fun of the pretensions and hypocrisies of mainstream society. This style was created by Lecoq and developed separately by Gaulier. It is very popular with young performers, particularly those involved in New Circus. Many of them are trying to survive at the fringes of the performing arts and quite rightly identify as outsiders if not as rejects. They may have experienced prejudice towards the world of beggars, travellers and the disadvantaged and are excited by the use of comedy as a weapon rather than the naive, sexless comedy of clowns. The huge success of Archaos in this country was in part due to their urban, streetwise adaptation of this style. A small group of practitioners in the South West of England – Jonathon Kay, John Lee and Franki Anderson have developed a synthesis of the Clown and Bouffon styles which they call Fool.

For myself I have used this style in two ways. The first way derived from the absurd, ritualistic games that are played by the buffoons; I used these as a basis for devising eccentric physical comedy. Max Wall's dances and John Cleese's walks are examples of the established popularity in Britain of this kind of comedy. Recently I have been looking at ways to develop this area in which the comedy is created purely through abstract movement particularly using contrast and juxtaposition.

The second way I have used this style was to take the buffoon rejection of conventional behaviour and use this in street theatre work in order to confront the public with their own limitations. When done well street theatre work can be a liberating experience for performer and public alike. My aim is to provoke the public into asking questions about my behaviour and by implication realise how constricted they are by conventions. One of the characters I play uses the actual buffoon costume I made at Lecoq's ten years ago. The buffoon hierarchy is frequently inverted so that the highest status king/queen becomes the lowest status baby and vice versa. As king I made a costume that used the materials of baby wear – white and pastel blues and pinks, dress-maker's scraps that I had found on the street. Attached to my elbows, wrists, knees and ankles are ribbon-covered extensions that transform the shape of the body, the belly is padded and the head is crowned with tripartite wedge-shaped extensions. The overall appearance is absurd, pretty but disconcerting. My function as I walkabout is to switch from commanding grandeur to childish petulance and playfulness. Women are amused by the spectacle. Small children can be terrified and older children can often be engaged in play. Young men, on the other hand, can find this figure very threatening because it clearly negates the values of masculinity and adulthood whilst being played by an adult man. At a street festival in Exeter I encountered a group of young men who directed homophobic abuse at me as they went past; choosing to play with this 'offer' I skipped after them trying to encourage the 'threatening game' that they had offered to play – the more they threatened the more I would parody play-act being afraid, lightly making fun of their macho behaviour. Being confused by this opposite reaction to the one to which they were used, they retreated and laughed it off except one who got me by the throat in a shop doorway. Because I offered no resistance and maintained an intelligent naivety, even praising his game-play, he made himself look ridiculous by threatening to punch this baby-like figure; to my relief friends dragged him off. They eventually went away deeply confused.

The other walkabout character I play looks very normal; a suit, spectacles, briefcase and umbrella make up the image of a minor office worker or sales representative. This discreet appearance makes possible invisible infiltration of the public. The drama becomes apparent when his behaviour becomes abnormal. Usually I find places to stand that are conspicuous, unusual and illogical such as inside fountains, ponds, litter bins or on the top of street furniture. The drama is created by the questioning of the public – they often approach and ask why I am standing in that place and I often respond with the Spike Milligan line – "We've all got to be somewhere", which gives them an answer but raises further questions. As far as possible I try to avoid talking and if they stand and stare I give them a look suggesting that it is rude to stare and that I do not see why they should find my behaviour so extraordinary. The drama is heightened when police or security guards arrive and insist I stand elsewhere and there follows a nonsense conversation about why some places are designated as suitable for standing and others are not. My refusal to acquiesce gathers a crowd who either enjoy this strange logic and who sometimes defend my position or who walk away shaking their heads mystified.

The crucial difference between Lecoq's school and that of Gaulier is the emphasis on devising. As a theatre writer and director, Gaulier prefers the traditional demarcations between writer, director and performer. Gaulier trains for performance not for dramaturgy. Lecoq on the other hand, used to be (and still occasionally is) a performer. He has been keen to re-establish the performer as the key source of creativity – the 'author-actor' as he calls it. The Moving Picture Mime Show and Théâtre de Complicité show this method to work well. The director's function is fulfilled from within the group rather than being imposed from outside. There have been some notable disasters when British Lecoq groups have worked with directors who have not shared the language, criteria and methods of Lecoq work or who have not understood the context in which the shows will operate.

The 'autocours' (self-teaching) aspect of the Lecoq course takes the form of weekly projects, devising to given specifications which are then presented and assessed. One learns the problems of group dynamics, develops an ability to propose and listen to ideas and also to identify other people with whom one shares similar tastes and aims. What became particularly useful was learning to try out everyone's ideas as they came up rather than editing ideas by discussion beforehand. In this way all the group stay involved in solving the presented problems. This is obviously much easier with small groups. With larger groups there is a necessary process of identifying leaders and followers.

When Lecoq-trained actors are involved in productions with a traditional hierarchy they can be frustrated by being denied their creativity by an unsympathetic director who may feel threatened by ideas coming up from lower down. A sympathetic director, on the other hand, will be glad of this input. Under Phillida Lloyd's direction the production of *Oliver Twist* at the Bristol Old Vic (in which I played the Artful Dodger), became an ensemble piece as the actors ran some of the rehearsal sessions and searched for physical ideas collectively. Because the actors feel responsible for the work and are concerned for the whole and not just their own part the shows will continue to develop during the run whether the director is present or not. This improvement is not merely in the sense of 'running-in' the show but actually expanding, diminishing or changing material.

The language, criteria and reference points that make it easy for Lecoq-trained performers to work together can also make it difficult for other performers and there is certainly a danger of forming an introverted clique. It was for this reason that I was keen to work with non-Lecoq people in Mummer&Dada. Our aim initially was simply to go out and enjoy the interaction with a real public on the streets and release ourselves from the exacting criteria at Lecoq's. Clear criteria are essential but it can also be beneficial to have a looser attitude rather than being straight jacketed by 'artistic correctness'.

4

THE THEATRE WHICH DOES NOT EXIST: NEUTRALITY TO INTERCULTURALISM

John Martin

The Challenge

It was the end of two years of hard slog; moments of inspiration, moments of confusion, constant challenges and personal disasters, sudden discoveries and long frustrations. After two years the journey was over – or was it?

On the final day at the Ecole Jacques Lecoq there was no graduation ceremony, it was very informal for the thirty of us who had survived the two tough elimination rounds from the hundred entrants. Lecoq chatted to us and then, in one of those moments of revelation which are his genius, came the phrase:

"I have prepared you for a theatre which does not exist.
Go out and create it."

The fact that it was so stirring for all present does credit to the greatness of a teacher who had instilled this spirit of curiosity, creativity and adventure in us all. Compared to all those drama schools (especially in Britain) which churn out actors in the style which the market demands, thus compounding the sclerosis of modern theatre, this was a challenge, a call to artistic arms.

Of course the cold light of the next morning brought hard reality. How **do** you create a theatre which does not exist? The need for the new revitalised theatre was clear, but the "how" is more difficult and has been occupying many of us ever since.

Lecoq had, however, given us the tools for the job, although it was never his way to show the model, rather to persuade each individual of his or her own capacity to create. There is no typical Lecoq student, for each one is encouraged along his or her own path, and this is another of his great talents. Lecoq graduates can be found along so many paths; in avant-garde theatre, as circus clowns or theatre clowns, teaching or performing mask work, as directors of movement in big national companies or drama schools, as directors, writers or stand-up comics, but each one is still taking up that first challenge.

I have no idea if Lecoq says the same thing to each departing group, but in some way he must have instilled the same desires and beliefs in all those who have passed through his school. Neither am I sure that I fully understood Lecoq and his priorities in the way others did. For me it is sufficient that I went to Paris quite simply wishing to hone my skills as a good repertory actor and I left with radically changed views, feeling myself to be part of a movement of theatre-makers which could contribute something new and help counter the Deadly Theatre everywhere (and especially in most British companies).

Influencing British Theatre

There is probably no other theatre tradition (at least in western culture) which is as resistant to change from outside as the British. There is probably no other theatre which is so arrogantly confident of its own superiority that it sees no need to look at other ideas to change its old (fashioned) ways. Britain is an island, its theatre insular. I still hear British theatre practitioners, directors, actors, teachers (and, of course, politicians) saying that we have the best theatre in the world but this has not been true for most of this century, if it ever was. Certainly within the western theatre tradition this century the movers and the shakers have come from Poland, the Soviet Union, France, Italy and the USA and most of these have remained unknown or ignored in Britain. (Yes, there is Peter Brook, but look which way he went.)

English actors, of course, are tremendously well trained for the theatre which exists in Britain, as market forces demand. I have never seen, anywhere in the world, actors who can so quickly pick up a text and find a reading, a cadence, a character, a believable performance, but this is interpretative and not newly creative in any deep sense. They are not trained to change theatre but to preserve it.

And so it was, when I returned to Britain from Lecoq, and when I auditioned in theatres around the country, that directors looked at me with blank puzzlement when I talked of his work. He was unknown, as were Grotowski and La Mama ETC with whom I had also worked, as were the names of Schechner, Beck, Kantor, Mnouchkine, Lavelli, Wilson and many more. A few university teachers knew of them but not the theatre leaders and makers, so nothing was changing and the talking heads ruled. It has changed now, a little, thanks to those like LIFT, Thelma Holt, Moving Picture Mime Show and Complicité, but don't be fooled, we are still largely ignorant of where the real cutting edge of theatre is at work.

I thank the British Theatre directors for their ignorance (although British Theatre shouldn't), for it stopped me wanting to be an actor in that system. If Lecoq had shown me the tools, the intransigence of British Theatre

John Martin in *Taxi Clowns* at Stockholm's City Theatre. Photo courtesy of John Martin.

showed me that changing it could not be done from inside by the actors. And so I became a director, a writer, a researcher and a trainer of performers. When British theatre attitudes have been too unbearable I have worked in theatre in France, Germany, Sweden, Belgium, Nigeria and India. In all those countries there is a desire and a curiosity for new work. In my early career people everywhere, knowing I was a Lecoq graduate, wanted me to teach them about his work; everywhere except in Britain.

The osmosis of Lecoq's ideas into British theatre is taking place, but very slowly. As more people pass through his school and return here the influence increases. The early work of Shared Experience, its *Arabian Nights*, with the wonderfully gifted Lecoq graduate Celia Gore Booth, was a breath of fresh air, and its style was the direct precedent for mainstream RSC's *Nicholas Nickleby*. The all-Lecoq Moving Picture Mime Show took that physical narrative a step further and broke open the definitions of mask and mime, and Théâtre de Complicité, although variable from production to production, have brought the physicality to literary text, in a way Lecoq certainly intends. For he insists, when people say his school is a mime school (using the word in a condescending, even derogatory, way).

"Mime is not a theatre where the actor does not speak, mime is theatre where the actor's body does speak."

His theatre is total, text and body, from Greek tragedy to Molière, to the modern avant-garde.

The Tools

None of the companies cited above are "pure" Lecoq. They, and many others, have been influenced by him and by many others researching in the field, whether his close colleagues like Pierre Byland, Monika Pagneux or Philippe Gaulier, or those like Grotowski, Brook and Mnouchkine who embody parallel paths. It is the ability to be inspired by many sources which has given them such richness. And yet Lecoq even prepares you for this multiplicity of influences. He wakes you up to all potentials.

Perhaps just as important as the methods he uses is the atmosphere of the school itself, in particular its internationalism. When I was a student there were twenty six different nationalities in the school from all five continents. This is a far greater mix than anyone (especially in insular Britain) normally works with, and it obliges everyone to re-examine their own traditions, and priorities as they share creativity with other peoples. Working in such an international body is one of the most exciting challenges for any artist.

Neutrality and Beyond

Primary in Lecoq's work is the training of the body as an expressive medium and this has been well documented elsewhere. But it is worth noting that he begins with a process to render each student "neutral". The subsequent retraining of the body from this base is never seen as a search for aesthetic beauty (as in much western dance); abjuring the use of mirrors the body is trained through experience from inside.

This concept of neutrality is central to his work, and is a state of great readiness and energy, not a state of non-presence. Neutrality is where everything is possible, not where everything has stopped, and many months are spent achieving it. It is a physical and mental state which is free of the little idiosyncracies of everyday life. To achieve this state is to be ready to create a character, a mood, a shape, without the baggage of the outside world. It is just the same as a painter preparing a clean canvas or a sculptor making sure the clay is free of lumps before work.

It is, of course, the antithesis of type-casting, where someone is chosen because they have the demeanour, the gait, the cadence required for a particular character. From neutrality you are clear and able to create in any direction. You have a state of energised awareness which is pre-expressive. Much later I realised that this is also the state of the Noh actor, the Kathakali actor and many other forms where the physical dynamic is trained to place the actor in a state of creative tension before the character is adopted.

Lecoq uses the neutral mask to achieve this state, a long and beautiful series of explorations, and then uses that neutrality to be the starting point for character, for play, indeed for all improvisation.

Although Lecoq criticises work which is too psychological it is wrong to assume that his work is external. On the contrary he seeks a truth of expression through a logic of the body's experience and trains that body to express its interior workings. Of course Lecoq is seeking an alternative to the all-pervasive Stanislavskian and post-Stanislavskian techniques, and it is part of a grand tradition in this century to find other theatrical truths than the rather dull realism which has dragged down Western theatre.

The real tools that Lecoq gives his pupils are not the individual techniques, however interesting they may be, but the approaches.

Having achieved the breakdown to neutrality, and having refused the Stanislavskian path, an extraordinary world opens up of associations, tensions, rhythms; a research where anything and everything is useful to the performer as a point of reference. This boundary-widening, de-blinkering, is vital and Lecoq castigates those who rely on old certainties and will not open up to what is all around them. It is this which struck me as vital, far more than the work on clowns, bouffons or pantomime blanche.

Throughout the two-year training Lecoq is constantly putting his students into creative situations. The "autocours" is a system whereby every week a theme is given and groups of five or six people work at the end of each day to find a way of interpreting the theme theatrically. The themes vary from realistic to abstract, but by the end of the first year thirty mini-presentations have been created and, every Friday afternoon, criticised by Lecoq and the students.

At the end of the first year a more in-depth small group research is undertaken. For this "enquête" each group must study a life-style and find a way to present it theatrically, not to re-present it as in life (the realist's path), but to communicate its essence through theatrical images. The life-styles vary widely, I remember emergency ward doctors, long distance drivers, "clochards", monastic orders, and many more.

The sum of all this work, which comes on top of a day of technical and improvisatory work, is to enable everyone to *make* theatre, find ways of communicating, and build in to it what has been learned in the class work.

The final tool is a model given by one special element of Lecoq's undoubted genius, that everyone has his or her own moment and his or her own direction of development. Watching him tease people out along their path, awaiting the right moment of maturity (sometimes after frustrating months) to goad them, or give them free rein, shows his deep experience and understanding. It is an object lesson for all theatre teachers and for directors.

A Personal Path

Some ten years after leaving Lecoq I was directing in India for the British Council. In traditional Indian learning everyone has a "guru" (a principal teacher, not necessarily a spiritual leader), and this is not only in the traditional forms like Kathakali, but also in modern theatre companies, where performers speak with love and respect of their guru. In turn I was asked who was my guru.

I had learned from many teachers of many skills (and still do), but there was no hesitation in naming Lecoq as my guru for I can draw a direct line from those ideas he instilled in me, to my reasons for working in India, and my reason for now directing Britain's leading intercultural performance company, Pan Project.

Even more wonderful – a few years ago (1988) I attended a lecture-demonstration given by Lecoq at the South Bank. I listened to him describing his work, his beliefs, his discoveries: things I have worked with and developed over many years. And I found myself disagreeing with much of what he said. Although I still use much of his work directly in mine, I have

John Martin as Dodu in *Alice in the Luxembourg Gardens* by Romain Weingarten,
Kings Head, Islington, London. Photo courtesy of John Martin.

taken it into new areas where it is re-examined by dint of applying it to new situations. Through this I have discovered new and different things. It was not a disappointment that I disagreed with him, I felt sure that he would have thoroughly approved, for it was his regime of questioning which, having inherited it, took me to this point.

It is not obvious how Lecoq could influence intercultural work in Britain. Indeed Lecoq was devoted to a purely European tradition of development and he often labelled other theatre forms as "folklorique" as they did not show the purity of expression he researched (although he retained a great admiration for Noh and Kabuki). But there is a very direct line of search and research for it must be true in modern Britain that Interculturalism is the Avant-Garde of today.

So how?

The technical and conceptual tools which Lecoq gave me led me to follow paths of developing physical theatre. This took many forms almost always unexpected ones:

One of the aspects which I had found most difficult at Lecoq was the concept of clowning. Lecoq, Fo, Byland and Gaulier had all pushed us into the ring to find the "bide", (literally, "flop"), the void in which the naked clown is born. At that time I didn't want to be a clown, I wanted to play Hamlet! I struggled with and struggled against it. I am sure, by the end, Lecoq agreed that I just wasn't clown material.

But then, whilst directing the International Theatre Workshop in Scheersberg in Germany, I met Polish director Helmut Kajzar who was developing his meta-daily theatre, and who was the favoured director of playwright Tadeusz Rózewicz. His work needed the open honesty and nakedness of clown play. The result was a production of Rózewicz's *The Funny Old Man* with four Lecoq graduates which played the ICA and then toured France, Germany and Poland. In it Kajzar made a rule for us: the performance was based on a number of children's games to be played genuinely with the text. Whenever anyone felt they were acting playing the game, rather than playing it, they had to go to the front of the stage, jump ten times, face the audience with "nothing" and then, with that mood, start playing the game again.

This was so close to what Lecoq's "bide" had demanded that all his clown work made sense immediately and made the show very successful. It subsequently led us to develop several clown shows with a new understanding and I found myself performing as a clown in a three-month engagement in Stockholm's City Theatre. Not what I expected!

In a similar way the mask work taught by Lecoq has had knock-on effects. Not only did I see its vital function in demanding physical levels of play from actors but it has enabled me to create works as diverse as a performance using the Basel larval masks for a touring production in

Dreams of Inanna at the International Theatre Workshop, Scheersberg, West Germany.
Director: John Martin. Photo: Tomas Steenborg

Lapland, chorus work in Greek tragedies in India (the chorus is another of Lecoq's favourite physical theatre forms), half-mask work to encourage communication in mentally handicapped children, or a production of Molière's *Malade Imaginaire* at London's Drama Centre using commedia (and commedia-influenced) masks. This last was with method-trained actors, the very antithesis of physicalisation – an interesting clash!

Later still, in an Intercultural Summer School in Masked Theatre from around the world, it was still the Lecoq work in neutral, Basel and half-masks which was the most appropriate familiarisation and sensitisation process before participants met mask forms like Noh, Topeng, Nyau and Dixi.

Improvisation

But the greatest element which has served in developing new work is the ability to structure improvisations from given material, whether this is finding a physical text to a written one, or taking one action and finding infinite variation on it, or developing precise body language expression through isolation and breathing.

This has been enormously useful in running workshops around the world and in finding rehearsal methodologies for some forty productions.

A great deal of mystique surrounds the concept of improvisation and many performers have a real apprehension when faced with it. This is understandable if the paths of creativity have not been made clear. An improvisation is a search in the unknown, and the unknown can be fearful. However if you know how to look for, how to feel and follow impulses and ideas which emerge from the neutral body, the journey becomes exciting. After the Lecoq training, and my own development and research, there was no longer any fear of creativity through improvisation, and it was much easier to pass on this way of working to my performers, who in turn produced ideas far beyond the possibilities of one director thinking about "what to do".

Indeed so much of the history of western physical theatre is rooted in the ability to discover new material through improvisation that the fact that British actors and directors are so little trained in ways of improvising must account for the low level of physical theatre in this country, or at least the low level of importance it has been given.

It was largely accident that brought me from a directing career in Germany, where these ideas were being developed, to Britain and a fascination for research in interculturalism. On returning to London the British Council asked me to visit India to run workshops on actors' creativity, to direct a production in Bengali with a prominent group from the Third

Josette Bushell-Mingo in Pan Project's *Under the Moon* at the ICA, London.
Director: John Martin. Photo courtesy of John Martin.

Theatre movement, and to attend an international conference on using traditional material in modern theatre.

The conference was an inspiration. There were many Indian experts in traditional and modern performance, most of them still unknown to me, Japanese experts like Tadashi Suzuki, and western experts like Schechner, Halpin and Barba. Barba was beginning his fascinating (although, I think, seriously flawed) Theatre Anthropology, Schechner was researching Indian theatre for his own productions and theories of interculturalism, Suzuki's use of Noh in his acclaimed *Trojan Women* was well known. Their Indian counterparts, Ratan Thiyam, Probir Guha, B. V. Karanth, Mrinalini Sarabhai, K. N. Pannikar, had gone just as far but they knew much more than their western colleagues. They knew that their own rich performance traditions did not have the almost impenetrable barriers, the iron curtains, between drama, dance, mime, mask, music etc. which we have. This, of course, gave them a much wider vocabulary for their work. No need to integrate into a "total theatre", it was already there.

The conference showed examples of new Indian theatre, rooted in traditional (sometimes centuries old) performance forms, but dealing with modern issues, or at least dealing with old themes in a modern way.

Where was Lecoq in all this? Quite simple. In watching modern Indian theatre of this type I was seeing again a strong physical theatre. At the time when the steam had gone out of the European and American physical theatre companies, largely for want of establishing rules and criteria by which to work, here was the growth of a performance style in which physicality had always been a strong part, and in which there was a methodology and aesthetic relating physical expression to text, to rhythm, to music etc.

In my workshops and productions which immediately followed this conference I was working with performers who had a strong knowledge of traditional forms and a clear idea of what they wanted to express in their work. There was only one element missing, which did not belong to their traditions, and where I was able to help. These performers needed the methods of improvisation to syncretise their vocabulary and adapt it for their own expression.

The resulting performance, *The Question of Abdul Hannan*, for Calcutta's Living Theatre was an eye-opener for me and a catalyst for my work in Britain.

What it showed was that the path of physical theatre, of Lecoq's "speaking body", could be inspired and invigorated by the study of richer and older theatre traditions from outside Europe. In setting up the Pan Cultural Performance Project, which later became Pan Project, the aim was to merge the rich vocabularies of non-western theatre with the traditions of improvisation and creativity which have marked the avant-garde in twentieth-century European Theatre. This is exciting, new, difficult work. It demands finding the performer's neutral presence (again) and then finding within it the sources of energy, flow, voice and expression which can be absorbed from other theatrical influences.

This is a movement which can make a major impact on the deadly theatre in Britain, for it brings back to the actor's vocabulary much of the celebratory richness which transcends the dull realism which has invaded our stages. It can bring back to theatre elements which film and television cannot inspire: the presence, the stamp of the foot, flash of the eye, resonance of heightened speech in space, rhythm of the body, the word, the gesture.

As well as enriching our experience, it strikes out for a theatre which reflects Britain's contemporary multi-culturalism, a theatre which should become much more relevant to cross-sections of society and which creates a common forum for actors of all ethnic groups. It is exciting because it moves, it has a physical text, actors work between words, around words and often without words. It appeals for all the reasons Suzuki gave in his demand for a rekindling of the muscular, animal energy which our techno-society has lost.

The artistic and political arguments for intercultural theatre which we take very seriously, are the subject of another article. In terms of Lecoq it is very fair to say that, firstly, I would not have been able to set up Pan Project if I had not had the tools of physical analysis and of creative synthesis from his work and training. Moreover in developing performances we have consistently found that our work has naturally become a theatre of physicality, mask, text and music. This has never been a conscious attempt to be "inter-disciplinary", it is the natural consequence of intercultural work. Whether it is Jacqui Chan's expertise in the body-tensions of Japanese theatre which aid her to hold the moment in *Dreams of Inanna* or *Under the Moon*, or it is Mallika Sarabhai using vocabulary of South Indian martial art, Kalaripayattu, to tell the story of Rani Laxmi in *Shakti – The Power of Women*, or Peter Badejo's adapting rhythmic speech from Indian story-telling in *Itan Kahani: The Story of Stories*, these cross fertilisations have brought richly successful elements to the productions we have created in Britain and toured around the world.

Whether in performances or in community projects, in one-person shows or research summer-schools, the curiosity and analysis, the improvisations and creativity that Lecoq engendered in me and my colleagues have had an effect on British Theatre which I am sure Lecoq would never have dreamed of.

The theatre does not yet exist, but it is coming.

Merci, Jacques!

5

THE MASKS OF JACQUES LECOQ

John Wright

Since founding his school in 1956 Jacques Lecoq has emerged as the most articulate exponent of a physical theatre. His influence is world-wide and more than any other teacher his work is at the heart of what Stephen Daldry views as 'an explosion of form in British theatre'.[1] The work of Steven Berkoff and Moving Picture Mime Show in the seventies and eighties did much to bring his work to a wider public attention and when I visited his school in Paris in 1990 more than half of his students were British. Today with the remarkable achievements of Théâtre de Complicité, with Philippe Gaulier, a former teacher at Lecoq's school, now basing his own school in London and with an increasing number of Lecoq-trained artists working in all aspects of our theatre it is safe to conclude that Lecoq's teaching is making its mark on British theatre practice. But what is this teaching with masks; where does it come from and why is it so special?

Lecoq's pedagogy has evolved through the systematic exploration of five masks: the neutral mask, the larval mask, 'le masque expressif' or character mask, the Commedia mask, and the red nose of the clown.

At first glance Lecoq's work appears to owe a great deal to Jacques Copeau. In the work of both men we can see the same fascination with the physicality of theatrical expression and a striking commitment to the play of the actor but the most obvious factor that links their work together is their use of the mask at the heart of their training process. Their choice of masks and even the order in which they use them appears to cover strikingly similar territory.

Copeau's Masks	Lecoq's Masks
The Noble Mask	The Neutral Mask
The non-figurative mask	The Larval Mask
The Character Mask	The Expressive Mask
The Commedia Mask	The Commedia Mask
The Personal Mask	The Red Nose

Lecoq's masks are used in the order listed above.
Copeau's masks were used in no particular order.

Between Copeau and Lecoq

In 1945 Lecoq worked with Jean Dasté[2] and his wife Marie-Hélène Copeau. (Dasté was an actor, director and a former teacher at the Vieux Colombier, Copeau's school.) Mira Felner writes: 'The Dastés tried to keep Copeau's spirit alive ... It is clear that the period with Dasté served as a departure point for the Lecoq techniques.'[3] But was it as simple as that? Certainly Lecoq does not think so: "When I started (he said emphatically) I had never heard of Copeau." Lecoq learnt the Copeau technique of using masks from Dasté but he was employed as a movement director with Dasté's company which implies that something of his 'technique', in an embryonic form, had already found its point of departure.

In both philosophy and approach Copeau and Lecoq could hardly be more contrasting. Copeau built a close and well-ordered residential community at the Vieux Colombier:

"He saw his role as being a spiritual guide, 'to filter, choose, balance, harmonise'. (His students') lives were to be dedicated to theatre through playing – celebrating birthdays, homecomings and other festivals."[4]

Lecoq, on the other hand is a confrontational teacher who works primarily through a form of 'via negativa' (the negative way). This is a strategy where the teacher restricts comment to the negative, namely what is *inappropriate* and unacceptable, thus forcing the student to discover what is *appropriate*, whilst avoiding being prescriptive.

Picture the scene with forty students facing a space and the teacher proposing a theme and asking: "Who would like to try?" It doesn't take much to imagine the size of this challenge. The students must find it in themselves to play with the theme in front of their peers with only a vague idea of what it is that the teacher is looking for. The teacher waits on the student's initiative restricting his or her self to the role of a mirror that speaks so at the end of each offering the student is likely to be told: 'That is not it. Thank you. Sit down. Two more people please.'

The via negativa is a tough but thorough learning process that compels each individual to find his or her own way in the work through watching, listening and eventually taking a risk in front of the audience. These are invaluable skills for a theatre artist which, in the devising process, have to be found under pressure. There is no theoretical discussion in this approach and little explanation. Lecoq habitually uses rich metaphorical language in an attempt to keep the work at the level of a passionate search.

By implication, anyone using the via negativa must know, or appear to know, exactly what they are looking for and to practitioners with no experience of this approach a number of questions inevitably spring to mind:

is Lecoq working from a base of clear and objective fact or is he working to serve a personal aesthetic? And to follow on from the last question: is he not in danger of creating a culture of correctness?

Lecoq uses the via negativa to manipulate creative energy. Sometimes he knows exactly what he wants his students to find and sometimes he simply uses it as a strategy to generate urgency; an atmosphere of white-hot discussion and experiment as his students struggle to find exactly what it is they think he is looking for. He plays a sophisticated game with his students and dislikes them being too comfortable or too confident: 'when a class didn't undergo a crisis, I created one artificially.'[5]

As a consequence of the pressures of this process less instinctive actors are in danger of confusing the idea of being appropriate for the notion of 'getting it right'. If actors are working to 'get it right' and think they have just been told that what they have done is 'right' then there is every chance that they will believe that they are 'right', thus creating a culture of correctness. This is most evident in working with students straight from the school who suddenly find themselves confronted with different processes and new applications of similar ideas; I have been told: 'you can't use a mask like that' or 'that's not clowning'. This is not a criticism of Lecoq so much as a fear that, like Stanislavski, Lecoq is in danger of falling victim to his own disciples.

Viewed from the safer and more conventional 'learn and apply' model of teaching more prevalent in British drama training or from the discursive model of the British universities the via negativa looks more like fascism than creative freedom. The irony is that the: "this is the way you do it, now try it with this approach" to training is likely to result in a greater orthodoxy than the groping in the dark process of the via negativa. Lecoq does not tell his students what he thinks is 'right' but rather establishes unspoken criteria for what he regards as effective. He leaves his students to voice the criteria for themselves. In refusing to tell them what to do and only commenting on what they have done he separates himself from discussion in order to focus attention on what is being created on stage. Questions of meaning or interpretation are not his concern. He is not interested what his students 'write' so long as what they do write is clear and effective theatre.

In making the teacher the sole authority the via negativa invests all critical responsibility in that teacher. Ironically in delegating responsibility in this way the student can find a new freedom in so far as he or she is left in no doubt as to the effectiveness of the work and is therefore free to concentrate on the search. Lecoq is not seduced by a culture of correctness – he will often criticise student's work as being 'scolaire' or too like the established model. On the occasion of the thirtieth anniversary of his school he erected a banner across the school courtyard reading: "Don't do what I do. Do what you do."

Lecoq's teaching clearly has different aims from those of Copeau. Lecoq is committed to the exploration of movement as the creative root of theatre making. Copeau sought to 'renovate' the theatre of his day and investigate the essence of acting. Copeau was working for a speaking theatre; to accommodate a classic text. Today Lecoq is working for a devised theatre and towards new theatre forms. The Dastés may have inspired 'the spirit of Copeau' in the young Lecoq, and doubtless articulated some key ideas, but the main inspiration behind Lecoq's work with masks came from an entirely different source.

Between Lecoq and Sartori

In 1948 Lecoq was invited to teach movement at the University of Padua Theatre School, and his reputation as a teacher began to blossom. In Padua he met Amleto Sartori. Sartori was a gifted sculptor and an inspired mask-maker. By analysing the renaissance techniques of binding books in leather, Sartori rediscovered the process for making leather masks. With this discovery Lecoq and Sartori embarked on a research partnership that lasted almost a decade. We must not underestimate the importance of this relationship when considering Lecoq's work with masks. In Sartori Lecoq had found a collaborator who was not only a brilliant craftsman but who also had a strong theatrical imagination. By working together through countless drawings and prototypes to the final exploration of a new mask in the studio, Lecoq and Sartori produced masks so specifically designed for their function that they were like precision tools.

Sartori's work first gained public recognition when Lecoq introduced him to the director, Giorgio Strehler and all three worked together on his famous production of *A Servant of Two Masters*. Lecoq was teaching at the Piccolo Theatre School in Milan. Strehler was having great problems with the masks he was using; being made of cardboard and glue they were simply dissolving in the actor's sweat. The actors constantly complained about them and often refused to wear them. Sartori spoke of the Commedia masks he had made for Lecoq and an important period of research was born.[6] Much of what we know about the physical technique of Commedia performance, the movement qualities of the masks and all our experiential understanding of the style comes from this single project. From fragmentary evidence and tiny shards of information from the local Italian dialect theatre, but more especially in exploring a set of effective masks of the tradition Lecoq, Sartori and Strehler were able to re-invent the form. They sifted what concrete evidence they could from the widest possible sources and filled in the gaps with their own invention. Characters like Tartellia were an entirely original creation. 'Commedia was a major French export', was Lecoq's ironic comment.[7]

Like Copeau, Lecoq was fascinated by the richness of Commedia dell'Arte , but unlike Copeau he had Sartori to help him realise it. Without Sartori it is unlikely that Lecoq's work would have developed in the way it did. Sartori and Lecoq were the first practitioners this century to explore the relationship between the form and the theatrical function of the mask. They went on to develop the neutral mask and the expressive mask and had many other projects in mind when Sartori died at the age of forty-six. Lecoq felt his loss deeply as this was one of the most creative associations of his career[8] and one that had opened up an entirely new avenue of work with masks and probably sowed the seeds of his most recent research with shape, space and emotion, known as the 'Laboratoire d'Etude du Mouvement' (LEM).

At its best Lecoq's school is as much of a laboratory as it is a training course and as a laboratory the work is constantly shifting in emphasis. No two courses are the same and the work is still evolving: 'our work moves in three directions simultaneously: deeper, wider and further forward.'[9] Because Lecoq's mask work has become the model for so many people in this country over the last ten years and because his precepts of stage movement evolving from his use of masks have become an important frame of reference, Lecoq's use of the mask deserves careful consideration.

The five key masks

Lecoq's process starts with the neutral mask. Essentially this is the same mask as Copeau's 'noble mask'[10] but by re-defining it as a 'neutral mask' Lecoq has developed an important concept that has become fundamental to his pedagogy as a whole. For Copeau the noble mask gave the actor the stillness and confidence to complete a movement. Lecoq's neutral mask takes this idea further; Sartori created a mask that has neither a history nor a future but simply lives in the moment, without comment.

The word 'neutral' needs some clarification. It does not mean 'neuter'. Lecoq uses both a male and female neutral mask (the male being slightly larger than the female). By neutral Lecoq does not mean 'uniform' either. We each have our own neutrality which is our essential physical self determined by our physique with all our personal traits, strains and conflicts removed. One of the first observations that a group of students tends to make when introduced to the neutral mask is that the same mask looks so different on each person in the group. It is not the mask that is different but the individual the mask reveals. Bari Rolfe, the American mask teacher and former student of Lecoq, has renamed the neutral mask the 'universal mask'. Others have called it a 'bland mask.' Neither of these words captures the delicate balance that Lecoq is trying to articulate. Neutral means: 'occupying a middle position between two extremes.'[11]

A typical theme that Lecoq may use as an initial exploration of the neutral mask is that of the mask waking up for the first time and seeing the world. Most students feel they must bring a story of wonder, or even fear to the action when all that is required is the simple action of waking up. There is no conflict in the neutral mask. It is never tired or ill but always in 'a state of equilibrium'. Because there is no conflict in the face, the neutral mask creates conflict in the minds of the audience who, on seeing the mask, sense that something is about to happen. By making no comment or by 'having no story', the neutral mask creates a vacuum that, as an audience, our imaginations rush to fill.

It is this profound economy of movement that makes the neutral mask dramatic. Lecoq believes that, once an actor is on stage with a body 'like a blank sheet of paper', then he or she can begin to see the world afresh from a state of unknowing. In that state, with all personal idiosyncrasies removed, he or she is physically open and available to gather knowledge about the world through the body.

The neutral mask captures a facial expression that is neither sad nor unduly happy but maintains a point of equilibrium. The mask captures an expression at the moment it is about to change. This equilibrium is reflected in the mask's design; Sartori's neutral mask appears to be symmetrical, the brows are relaxed and rounded, and the mouth is ready to smile, swear, eat or kiss but is doing none of these things. In making this mask Sartori was inspired by the young girl mask from the Japanese Noh theatre: *Ko omote*. In both masks we see a mouth that could be about to smile, kiss or swear but doing none of these things. Both masks capture a facial expression that is on the cusp between equally powerful feelings.

Lecoq is not interested in *expression* in this work but rather the reverse. He uses the neutral mask to enable his students to work with such openness and availability that the world can make an *impression* on the body. 'When the neutral mask sees the sea it becomes the sea'.[12] To put it in another way, in the neutral mask the Actor is able to let a clear image of the sea make a corporeal impression on him or her. The impression inspires a gesture, and the gesture will eventually inspire feeling.

"The fire which I see can flame in me. I can know that fire and when I identify with it, and play at being fire I give my fire to the fire."[13]

For Lecoq, we gain knowledge about the world through our ability to identify with the world and we achieve this through our sensory impressions. As a mask with no history and with no prior knowledge of the world, the neutral mask brings the student to a state of 'unknowing'.

The neutral mask is a constant point of reference in the first year work at his school and his students are led through a range of exploratory figures such as:

Neutral man meets neutral woman for the first time.

The neutral mask runs through the forest and discovers the plain.

The neutral mask sees a tree, sees a bird in the tree and sees it fly away.

To be clear, credible and effective, all these figures require an actor not only to find the corporeal impression of the image but also to place the image in space in such a way that the audience can 'read' it clearly.

Students progress through these initial experiences to further exercises in rediscovering the world by the study of elements, materials, objects, animals and even colours. These studies lead to such themes as 'fire man' meets 'water woman', 'paper woman' meets 'oil woman' and so on. Clear external references such as these enable the actor to discover a precise movement quality that, once captured, inspires a change in feeling.

In applying the neutral mask to such a broad range of external references, Lecoq confronts his students from the very start of his training with a bold physical canvas which offers strong emotional connotations. 'To give (your) fire to the fire' is the result of a somatic impulse. For example: when we try to make ourselves cry or sleep we consciously create within ourselves the appropriate physicality to induce the feeling. This is a somatic impulse. On stage, a somatic impulse occurs as soon as a 'fire person' is placed in a dramatic context. If you ask a 'fire person' to look for a lost key or 'a clay person' to run for a bus, the external reference will start to become internalised with surprising intensity.

In emphasising a physical understanding of the world around us and using that understanding as an external reference, Lecoq is giving his students a means of finding material with which to make theatre. External references are an infinite source of dramatic inspiration. The essential lesson behind this work is: 'tout bouge'; everything moves. Shapes inspire movement. Elements, materials, objects, space, sounds and colours can, according to this theory, imprint themselves on our bodies and inspire somatic impulses precisely the same way as a mask. Wherever we are our surroundings have the potential to become a source of corporeal inspiration for character action and narrative. We can see the fire, become the fire, and become the fire person. Lecoq is teaching a process of mimesis and for him this is the touchstone of instinctive writing.

'Le masque expressif' is essentially a character mask; a mask that appears to capture a clear personage; the face of a person at the moment of being condescending or at the moment of being stupid. Unlike the neutral mask this is a face in conflict. It may be the face of an idiot, an old man, a disgusted person or a beautiful woman. The term 'masque expressif' suggests the shift in emphasis in the physical dynamic of this mask. If the neutral mask facilitates corporeal impression, then the expressive mask requires the student to work with the opposite dynamic. Here the student must find the game of the mask and play it out to the audience. Lecoq emphasizes the rapport between the actor and the mask. For the mask to come alive we must see the game and the game releases the actor's corporeal *expression*.

The lesson of the neutral mask, however, is not far away If the mask is to make a corporeal impression on the actor's body then the actor must approach *le masque expressif* in a state of unknowing, with no preconceived ideas about the face he or she is about to assume. In this way the impulse can be discovered. Lecoq describes the relationship between the neutral mask and the expressive mask as follows:

"The neutral mask is not a surface mask but comes from deep inside one. The neutral mask is like the bottom of the sea: it's quiet, it's still. The expressive mask is like waves; underneath is the neutral mask"[14]

Compared with the expressive mask, the neutral mask is a much deeper experience. Under the expressive mask the student has the opportunity to hide behind the personage. Under the neutral mask the student must reveal his or her self without customary physical attitudes of apology or over-compensation.

The game of playing the expressive mask becomes more intense with the introduction of the *counter-mask*. In playing 'the idiot' as 'the intellectual' we begin to expose a humanity in the mask and to transcend type. If you assume the expression of a smile and then play an action of deep sadness, you will begin to get a taste of the game of the counter-mask. It is an idea that opens up a much wider game for the actor that goes beyond the immutable expression of the mask to a fascinating world of dramatic tensions where we realise that the snivelling victim can also be a bully or the matronly looking woman can be sexy. Through the counter mask it becomes clear that an effective mask is capable of the whole range of human feelings and that the challenge is to find the appropriate dramatic context to trigger the game.

To inspire more imaginative games from his students and, more importantly, to escape the restrictions of realism, Lecoq uses a non-figurative mask he calls the 'larval mask'. This mask is devoid of human features so there is no specific characterization suggested by it. Basically the larval mask is an unpainted Swiss carnival mask from Basel which in its plain white form suggests a face whose features are just about to come into being. They are called larval masks because they suggest a face covered in larvae which makes us begin to reconstruct the hidden features. Larval also derives from a Latin word meaning ghost or spirit. Lecoq began his early work with these masks by asking the question: 'What kinds of movement correspond to these masks? What space, rhythm, speed and direction?'[15] The minimal and often bizarre shapes that we see in the mask become completely acceptable once the student begins to follow the impulse of the shape. As with a cartoon character, we begin to accept the larval mask as a credible personage.[16] The semi-abstract shapes of these masks take the student into a different world from either the neutral mask or the expressive mask.

If you lift your eyebrows up as far as you can, you will assume an expression of amazement. In many of the larval masks it is as if the eyebrows have risen up so high that they appear to have slid off the face completely and the mask is locked in a state of perpetual astonishment. For this reason some people call them 'naive masks'. Unlike the neutral mask we see no perspective of learning about the world here. The larval mask discovers the world but does not necessarily make any sense of it. Like very small children, they blunder into things and what they don't understand they make up. The larval mask can be mercurial and potentially anarchic in a most endearing way, but the outstanding characteristic of this mask is its insatiable appetite for play.

With the larval mask Lecoq confronts his students with the task of finding the corporeal impression from a shape. A rounded blob-like shape will move in an entirely different manner from a sharp pointed shape. The larval masks require sensitivity rather than precision, and games rather than accuracy. These masks define their own world where, in a child-like way a cushion could become a mountain or a chair a horse. In the world of the larval mask nothing is what it appears to be and anything is possible.

Like Copeau, Lecoq teaches the commedia dell'arte as a reference. Whilst encouraging his students to respect the form he is not interested in period authenticity. 'I don't bury myself in historical references.' He uses commedia as a means of integrating physical work and vocal expression. This is the moment in the course where the word meets the gesture and 'the scream seeks the sign'. In other words the actor must find the appropriate voice for the physically of the mask. In their research into the commedia masks Sartori and Lecoq evolved masks with a clear animal motif such as a dog or a cat Arlecchino or a cockerel Captain or a hen Punchinello. The masks are highly stylised with angular features which at first glance look nothing like a human face. The scenarios and lazzi conspire to take each of the characters to the point of physical extremes; the ultimate point of despair. For Lecoq, commedia is 'human comedy'. He attempts to reveal the humanity of the farce by which he means the comedy of ridiculous individuals locked together in what is for them a desperate struggle. We laugh at what they do and we laugh at what they look like because we can all see in that ridiculous personage something we recognise in ourselves. The challenge for the actor here is to find his or her version of a character apparently fixed in a highly stylised form and to be credible in a style that moves at breakneck speed, with sudden shifts in rhythm.

The final and most important mask in Lecoq's training is the red nose of the clown. Copeau was instinctively drawn to the Fratellini Brothers (a troupe of circus clowns) and invited them to his school, only in the end to feel dissatisfied with the set nature of their routines. Lecoq has discovered in the red nose the final point of masking for his students. This takes the form of the discovery of one's personal clown, that child-like idiot inside every one of us which we try so hard to cover over with our social masks of skill, education, authority and sophistication. To find the clown, Lecoq brings his students to a point of psychic nakedness. He calls it 'Le Flop' (or "le bide"). Interestingly Pierre Byland calls it 'the fiasco', while Gaulier calls it 'the void'. It is that catastrophic moment when the audience realises that the situation is irretrievable but the Clown, despite the odds, still hopes to rescue the situation.

One of Lecoq's initial exercises in Le Clown is for the actor to burst on stage and take an exuberant and enthusiastic bow anticipating rapturous applause, only to realise that the audience are wholly indifferent to him. In the realisation of this preposterous mistake we see 'Le Flop' in the actor's eyes and the little mask of the nose directs our attention to them. We want to look behind the nose to see who it is that looks so stupid and we find ourselves looking into the actor's eyes. The red nose becomes 'a tiny neutral mask for the clown.'[18] The actor is confronted with the daunting challenge of self-revelation. To study the Clown is to study yourself. For the actor, this is the greatest challenge and Lecoq believes it to be the greatest freedom and the most complete expression of the absurdity of the human condition.

Between Lecoq and his protégés

Each mask that Lecoq uses brings with it its own imaginative world and its particular dynamic and quality of release. When explored in sequence these five masks constitute a course in creative freedom. Different generations of Lecoq students have taken different aspects of his work and made pieces with whatever theme has particularly inspired them. In the late seventies Mummenschanz developed the larval mask into their own unique style of theatre using body masks and structures completely encasing the actor. They evolved a new theatrical language out of the animation of shapes and the manipulation of materials. They made a drama out of a giant ball trying to roll on to a plinth and created a love scene where a couple ate each other's faces.

In England The Moving Picture Mime Show used the larval mask to create pieces like: *The Examination* and *Handle with Care* (both made in the late seventies). These pieces have become classics and were the first modern mask theatre productions to tour extensively in England The work of The Moving Picture Mime Show was the inspiration of Trestle Theatre Company. Trestle took the idea of the larval mask but created a style of character mask by making the faces more figurative in order to define specific types. *Crèche* (1981) and *Plastered* (1983) established Trestle as the leading mask theatre company in the country. *Plastered* was the first full length visual farce and toured nationally to considerable critical acclaim. During a run in London Simon McBurney and Marcello Magni of Théâtre de Complicité came to see the show and in spite of the gales of laughter from the audience they had strong reservations about the piece. Simon had problems with some of the masks but especially with the 'smallness' of the playing. It was not until a year or so later when I started to explore the non-figurative larval mask for myself that I realised why. In making masks that represented definite types Trestle had lost the ambiguity of the non-figurative shape which enables the actor to work on an extremely broad level of play and instead we had trapped ourselves at a level of physiological realism demanding small and intricate detail. The power of *The Examination* and *Handle With Care* lay not only in the credibility of the masks but in the size of the movement and the resulting range of play the masks afforded the actors. This was the reason behind Lecoq's use of the larval mask. Moving Picture Mime had simply taken the form and made a piece. This is a common trend in many Lecoq groups; to turn a pedagogical device into a theatre form. We can see the same trend in the work of Brouhaha whose clown pieces like *Whatever the Weather* (1993), have taken the device of the red nose and the stupid costume to create a style of imagistic theatre form the same devices that Lecoq was using in his teaching to reveal humanity and vulnerability.

Simon McBurney and Marcello Magni of Complicité steeped themselves in Lecoq's training and went on to further training with Phillipe Gaulier. Their early work like *A Minute Too Late* made in the early eighties, drew freely on Lecoq's teaching as a whole. In this piece we can see different levels of play such as: Clown, Commedia, Pantomime and Melodrama tossed together like a salad to make a short piece of theatre rich in sudden changes of rhythm and flights of fancy. Complicité may occasionally use masks in training workshops but they have never felt the need to produce a piece of masked theatre. Their ability to consolidate Lecoq's teaching rather than reconstitute its pedagogical forms has led to the astonishing achievements of their mature work, like *The Street of Crocodiles* (1993) and *The Three Lives of Lucy Cabrol* (1994). Both these productions emerge from an assured, sophisticated and eclectic level of play that is capable of creating indelible imagery and huge shifts of feeling.

Some Conclusions

The Lecoq school produces artists as diverse as the people themselves. The training he delivers uses the mask as a key for each student that can open the door to their creative impulses. His process offers arguably the most challenging and imaginative course in Europe that is a unique grounding for a theatre maker but as a pathway for an actor it is incomplete. A highly creative individual with an articulate and responsive body is only part of what is required in an actor. To produce a performer without an equally responsive voice and an imaginative response to language is like training a pianist to only use one hand.

The first three masks in Lecoq's training are full masks and the work covered in these masks is silent. The neutral, larval and expressive masks constitute a course in movement analysis, imaginative engagement, and play,[19] but why does Lecoq deny any systematic vocal reference in this work? He would probably argue that he is seeking to give the representation of life a poetic energy and that some level of constraint is indispensable in training an actor. Too much constraint will lead to virtuosity or an imposed aesthetic and too little 'to a soup of naturalistic gestures'.[20] However many students still leave his school with poor vocal skills.

If the neutral mask has a somatic influence on the body that same impulse can be sustained once the mask has been removed. Used in this way, the mask can have a similar influence on the voice. The voice requires the same muscular control as any other moving part of the body and is subject to the same idiosyncratic habits and personal clichés. All great voice teachers like Kristin Linklater and Frankie Armstrong, Cicely Berry or Patsy Rodenburg maintain that the body and the voice are inextricably linked; the observation has become a truism. I can understand the role of silence in renewing the importance of the gesture, but does speech always overshadow the gesture?

Lecoq has introduced more vocal work into his course over the last few years but without systematic preparation it could hardly be argued that it is sequentially built into the course. The fact that many of his students may go on to seek work in the 'speaking theatre', to use his own term, is not his concern. He runs a school in stage movement and not a theatre school. The five masks at the centre of his teaching provide an imaginative base from which to approach the corporeal roots of theatre and he teaches these roots as a series of six physical levels of play that occur either singly or in interaction with each other. These levels of play are: psychological realism, tragedy, melodrama, commedia dell'arte, clown and bouffon.[21] Written text is used largely as an application or development of a particular level of play. He makes no attempt to explore the 'neutral voice', for example, or 'the vocal counter mask'.

The real debate here is not about the extent to which an actor should speak but rather: what constitutes an actor's text? Lecoq's teaching with the mask has demoted the primacy of the written text but at the same time it has promoted the idea of a text of actions as being just as resonant and meaningful as carefully structured written language. Before the age of video the visual aspects of performance were always the most ephemeral. The great American clown, Emmett Kelly, for example, is remembered for an act which apparently consisted of eating a cabbage and crying. As a description of what actually happened this is meaningless. The fact is that Emmett Kelly's visual text has been lost.

By means of the mask Lecoq teaches the actor to write a text of actions and in liberating theatre from the bounds of literature his teaching celebrates the actor and the director as the authors of the piece but there are dangerous pitfalls here. Although we can make a clear, engaging and resonant piece of theatre entirely out of action, the more the work becomes the idiosyncratic authorship of an individual actor, the less transferable that work becomes as a piece of theatre. Once we lose the independent code of a text, be it physical or written, like trying to do a stage version of a Charlie Chaplin film, re-creation is reduced to imitation and the work is likely to become trapped at the level of mime. I do not use the word 'mime' in a perjorative sense. Mime is an essential element of theatre making; play, the somatic impulse and the use of external reference and the process of the mask itself are all mimetic disciplines. The written text transcends the mime by virtue of the fact that it is transferable; it is capable of constant re-creation and re-interpretation.

Lecoq maintains that mime is a transient form that emerges when theatre is in a state of decline. For Lecoq mime is a means of returning to the essence of theatre and of finding new beginnings. Lecoq does not run a mime school. His teachings, that we move before we think and that what we do on stage is more important than what we say, are lessons fundamental to good theatre practice and not the specialist preserve of the mime. It is a process that has little to do with words and at its best enables the actor to generate rich and allusive movement from apparently nowhere.

During the last fifteen years theatre training in England has lost touch with the demands of a theatre practice that has been gradually moving away from the 'actor as interpreter' to the 'actor as creator'. There are few institutions in England with the relevant expertise capable of offering a structured course in devising for the theatre and even fewer colleges offering a cohesive physical training for an actor. It is hardly surprising therefore that so many aspiring British artists seek their training in Paris. At a time when genre is being broken down and there is a determined shift away from the written word in theatre Lecoq is the only teacher offering a non-formalist and instinctive way of writing for the theatre.

The divergent tracks of actor training inspired initially by the pioneering work of Copeau and Stanislavski have today become known as physical and psychological theatre respectively. There is no point in labelling theatre as physical, psychological, political, spiritual, black or women's theatre. All theatre is physical and a healthy theatre will be all of these things. In using the mask to teach the making of theatre and in training the body at the expense of the voice Lecoq has deliberately created a dangerous imbalance in our theatre. He has 'made a crisis' in a theatre that had become too comfortable and too safe, and without having in mind precisely what he is looking for, he challenges us all to find another way.

Notes

1. See Simon Murray's essay above.
2. For more detail on Lecoq's influences see *Le Théâtre du geste*, Bordas, Paris 1987, p. 108.
3. Mira Felner, *Apostles of Silence*, Fairleigh Dickinson, Associated University Presses, 1985, p. 146.
4. James Roose Evans, *Experimental Theatre*, Routledge & Kegan Paul, London 1984.
5. As quoted by Leabhart, *Modern and Post-Modern Mime*, Macmillan, London 1989 p. 94.
6. Copeau had explored Commedia but his research was not as thorough. He used Commedia more as a reference. Strehler was attempting a revival of the form.
7. Lecoq. Interview with the author, March 1994.
8. Ibid.
9. Ibid.
10. Ibid.
11. *The Shorter Oxford English Dictionary*, Oxford University Press, 1977.
12. Lecoq. Author's workshop notes taken from London International Workshop Festival, 1985.
13. Jacques Lecoq. *Théâtre de la Ville*, no. 15 (January 1972, p.9).
14. Lecoq interview with Sears Eldredge August 1974. Appendix to Ph.D thesis *Masks: Their Use and Effectiveness in Actor Training Programs* Michigan State University, 1975.
15. Ibid.
16. These masks are the inspiration of Mummenschanz, a company of former students of Lecoq who have developed the larval mask into body masks and abstract creations which for all their abstraction still inspire a sort of anthropomorphism in the audience.
17. As quoted by John Rudlin in *Commedia dell'Arte*, Routledge, London 1994 p.201.
18. Lecoq. Interview with the author, March 1994.
19. Lecoq encourages his students to make their own masks and to adapt found objects into masks such as plastic containers or household objects. Industrial or sporting masks are also used in the first year work and have a similar function to that of the Larval mask.
20. Lecoq, *Théâtre du geste*, Bordas. Paris 1987 p 99.
21. Bouffon is a form of grotesque chorus that Lecoq evolved during the sixties to inspire an imaginative release through a process of hiding behind a ridiculously grotesque disguise.

6

"AMUSEZ-VOUS, MERDE!": THE EFFECT OF PHILIPPE GAULIER'S TEACHING ON MY WORK AS AN ACTOR AND WRITER

Victoria Worsley

I can still see Philippe's weary eyes on the afternoons when it seemed that his lumbago was particularly bad as he sat hunched over his drum and I'll never forget the terror that I might be the wretched performer doing some exercise up there in front of the rest of the class at whom despair forced him to shout "Amusez-Vous, merde!". It was often accompanied by a general (and to me terrifying) reminder that accountancy was a better profession for someone who couldn't have fun on stage. It wasn't a tactic guaranteed to put a performer at their ease and fill them with the required spontaneous sense of fun (nor was it very polite to accountants) but in essence it was absolutely the best advice that could ever be given and it has definitely been the element of Philippe's teaching that has affected my work the most. If there is no joy on stage there is nothing. Even in tragedy there needs to be a certain joy in the performance of it. It might sound basic but it is not generally taught as such and perhaps as a consequence it is surprisingly rare to find real pleasure in the theatre. I learnt a number of techniques and skills from Philippe which have affected my work and which I will also discuss but all of it seems to me rooted in this one essential principle: **enjoy yourself.**

Before pursuing my theme I should put myself in context. I studied with Philippe Gaulier and Monika Pagneux when they were still teaching together in Paris. I went for the first time ten years ago. Philippe teaches in a workshop format so it is possible to work with him for a month or two at a time which allowed me to continue to study with him over a period of a couple of years even while I was at University. I didn't manage to do all his courses and I know that some have been added since but I was only seventeen when I started and Philippe's teaching therefore helped to actually form the way I think about theatre and determine the direction my work has gone in. I had acted in largely conventional school theatre and at University began by playing lead roles in the Oxford University Drama Society plays and might therefore have trodden the usual route into a straightforward acting career. However, an interest in mime that began while

I was still at school led a friend to suggest that I help stage-manage for a company from the Lecoq school at the Edinburgh Festival one summer holiday which in turn led to my discovery of Philippe's teaching. As a result of what I was learning in Paris (and an early opportunity to work with director/writer/performer Neil Bartlett who had some common ground with Philippe) I set up Tattycoram Theatre Co. with three like-minded women who all subsequently trained with Philippe. Our first show was directed by performance artist Annie Griffin who has her own distinctive agenda but who has also absorbed some elements of the Lecoq/Gaulier teaching. We toured successfully for three years and I also toured two solo shows of my own.

In the last three years I have chosen to write rather than devise (the favoured process of most Lecoq/Gaulier-influenced companies) and have developed a more conventional acting career alongside, but I still carry Philippe's teaching with me. I find myself drawn by a combination of the emotional, psychological (and sometimes political) emphases more conventional theatre can offer and the theatrical language, skills and values of Lecoq/Gaulier inspired work and therefore cross between the two and don't belong to either quite. It is possible to take an anti-intellectual stance from Philippe's teaching as a result of his emphasis on "play" (and many companies do, fitting in with the trend in conventional theatre at the moment for "telling the story" above any consideration of what that might mean) but it isn't a necessary conclusion (Philippe himself is far from anti-intellectual). An actor needs not to be intellectual at the time of performing but the structure of a piece and the role of the performer within it can be. This area where the two meet is, to me, the most exciting place to be. I shall not be discussing the other aspects of my work in any depth here but shall indicate how I operate in that area to some degree as I go.

To come back then to the principle of **pleasure** what Philippe tried to elicit from us was something like the sparkle a child has when they are inventing a new game or just playing tag or even when they are simply aware that they are being watched. (Monika Pagneux also focuses on the delight and ease of invention children have.) It is an immediate pleasure arising directly out of the ideas, sensations and excitement of the moment as it arrives. Such pleasure is an engrossing and delightful thing to watch. An actor's pleasure is similar. There is the pleasure of doing something simply because it is enjoyable; the pleasure of inventing with other people and having to keep a scene afloat with ideas, jokes and feelings that arrive spontaneously; that of literally playing ball with lines, gestures, rhythms, looks and of course that of doing it all for an audience who can enjoy it. For an audience, a performer's pleasure can be infectious like that of a child, and even in conventional theatre there is praise for the actor who is "in the moment". This is all obvious in a way, but it places the emphasis on a different aspect of performing to the usual method school idea of an actor performing by digging into their personal and therefore often isolated experiences and working to render a line with emotional truth. I do feel that the latter approach is an important part of the work I do as an actor, but to me it is only half the story: if the engagement and sense of "play" is not there with the other actors and the audience then there is still nothing however deep the actor has dug into his/her emotions. Although a naturally good performer may just have pleasure on stage without ever articulating what they do, it is astounding how many actors do not and are suspicious of the whole idea. Working with the sort of actor who is locked up in themselves and has no pleasure in what they do or cannot share is a frustrating experience and can be equally frustrating to watch. For them, acting is (and looks like) work. However, ironically, I have also noticed that such a performer will often not just get by but even be welcomed and lauded. I would argue that this is because there is a strong ethic in some areas of the theatre and its audience that one shouldn't enjoy oneself too much at a play or it can't be serious Art and must be lacking in profundity. I am not suggesting here that serious work is bad and that all plays should be light weight or funny but that however grand, however tragic it is, a truly great piece of work carries itself lightly: it can take off, reach the ceiling with ease and even beyond rather than dragging itself along bound by chains of difficulty and "work", threatening to grind to a halt or crash through the floor under its own weight. This principle has affected me deeply as an actor and a writer.

As an actor, if you say you trained with Philippe Gaulier most people in traditional theatre expect you to want to jump about, stand on your head and pull faces. Not so. One effect his teaching has had on me when I am working as an actor on a conventional play is to help me develop a lightness even with the saddest of texts, an openness to the audience, an ability to connect with the quality of another actor's performance and a willingness to share a scene with my fellow performers in "play" terms.

As a devisor and writer it has affected me in a number of ways. Tattycoram made a name for itself partly because of the developed play relation between the three of us. By the end of our time together we had a scene in which, sitting on the floor and unable to see each other we breathed simultaneously, holding every in-breath (including a sharp, long one in the middle), for exactly the same time and letting each breath out at exactly the same speed. It sounds simple but it is surprising how few conventional companies can achieve that kind of thing as a matter of course. It is not something done by counting, the actors have to listen and be totally in tune with each other. In this country there is tendency to think that wonderful ensemble play means clapping in time or having a small cast play lots of parts. Philippe's teaching led me to see ensemble play as being able to respond to each other's timing, make the least gesture together automatically, breath together; as being able to catch an idea like a ball, play with it in turn then throw it lightly to the next actor, never letting it drop.

Tattycoram had fun on stage. Devising a new show often began not only with discussions about what the piece was about, but also with each of us confessing the strange things we most wanted to do on stage, be it wearing a particular dress or doing a turn as a man or singing a Tom Jones number sor whatever but, strangely, these odd desires often turned out to contain a lynch-pin for the meaning of a piece. For example, in my solo show *Make Me a Statue*[1] (devised with and directed by Caroline Ward) about the famous sculptor Camille Claudel, also lover of Rodin, I was absolutely determined to crash through a wall on a horse and sing the commendatore's part in the penultimate scene of *Don Giovanni* when the statue of the dead commendatore arrives for dinner. It's not quite as ridiculous as it sounds in that I do have an operatic training (and the horse and the wall did go by the board pretty early on) but after a long period of failing to find its place in the show it turned out to be the finale. By that point we had decided that I needed to be painted like a statue for the entire show and that the heart of the piece turned on Camille's contradictory position as both maker and model, as pedestalized possession and artist in her own right. The appeal of the statue at the end therefore fitted beautifully for a woman who felt that she had been robbed of herself as an artist by her work for Rodin and her relationship with him. In particular the statue's speeches are largely requests to be listened to (*Ascolta!*) and for answers (*Rispondi me*) which in my piece were addressed to two eight-foot copies of Rodin statues which were resolutely deaf and dumb throughout the show. The piece contained many other resonances which I do not have room to discuss here but it worked very well not least because I got to perform a tragic finale which I had huge pleasure in doing. The contextualisation and use of a piece like that has little or nothing to do with anything I learnt from Philippe but the impetus to perform what I enjoy doing did come from him and fusing that principle with the other concerns I have in my work has always helped to provide some of the most interestingly lateral and theatrical elements.

At one post-show discussion for Tattycoram I remember a woman who was familiar with our work saying that she enjoyed our shows because it always felt to her like we had come together to play games. She was more right than she knew. This is another way in which not just our performing but the way we found the building blocks of a scene and sometimes the entire structure of a show were influenced by this aspect of Philippe's teaching. Often an improvisation for a scene would start with someone saying, "OK, the game goes like this..." Very simple rules would follow. These games provided a simple, enjoyable and highly theatrical means of expression which could then be contextualised or have text added to make pieces of considerable sophistication. Again the latter process was not something we learnt from Philippe but was how we used some of his techniques. (In describing pieces here they will lose much of their sophistication which partly came from the resonances they had which were built up through the show but I will describe what I can.)

In *Make Me a Statue* there was a scene which started as a game in which I had to pretend my body was made of fluid lead and incredibly heavy. It began with me lying down on the floor, trying to reach a piece of clay on a plinth the other side of the room and turned into an entire slapstick routine whereby the joke was that I never could quite touch it. Looking at it, it began to feel like a piece about not being able to work and so then a text started to come out of it as well which, while still being part of the game, added a layer of information about the things you do to avoid work or the feelings you might have when you feel too low to create. The result was a very entertaining piece which also pin-pointed a certain feeling very well.

In *The Very Tragical History of Mary Shelley*[2] which was our first piece and which Annie Griffin was largely responsible for, there was a section called "the book game". It was literally that. The three of us stood shoulder to shoulder in the middle of the stage. We each had an open hard-backed book. Someone would start the game by slamming their book shut. We then all had to run and hide our book somewhere on stage or even in the audience and come back to our places at centre stage. Together we shut our eyes, hid our faces in our hands and counted to ten. On ten, we ran as fast as we could to find any book except our own and rushed to get back to our places. The first person back could read a bit out of the book until someone else slammed theirs shut. Then the other two had to shut theirs and the game started again. Literally, then, a book game. Nothing was set in terms of where the books were put or who read what, we just timed it together and literally played the game. The audience loved it for that play energy. It was utterly in the moment. Contextualise the piece and it becomes quite clever. We were all dressed in silk dresses playing Mary Shelley as a child. The setting was her father's study and the books were technical, informational books on the whole. Suddenly you have a piece about a woman trespassing on male territory reading by stealth, enjoying learning and hiding it as well as a subtext about elegantly dressed women behaving energetically and inelegantly. This game structure is something which Annie Griffin uses often in her work but I responded to it also as a development of Philippe's pleasure principle.

In the writing that I do now I still ask myself continuously, "What is the game?" In my play *And All Because The Lady Loves* …[3] I thought of sections in terms of games. "This is the bit when the game is that the telephone is her lover"; "The game here is that she wants to leave the room but she keeps having ideas that she wants to tell us"; "This is the bit when she has to pile all the contents of a table set for a romantic dinner *à deux* on top of each other in a fragile tower and make serious conversation with her lover at the same time, while the words of the romantic song in the background keep popping out of her mouth to her horror". This last plays very simply although its structure in terms of games is complicated because there are several things going on at once. I like it as a non-pedestrian and entertaining way of getting to some very difficult emotional situations. It also uses the languages of music and image as well as text which I like as a profoundly theatrical means of expression. Again the application is probably not something that Philippe would ever envisage, but the principles of game playing I learnt from him.

My current play, *Night-Train*, which is in its final draft stage, is entirely structured on games but in a far more complicated way. It is about a man and a woman in the street in the middle of the night. She has a suitcase. The entire action of the play is the games they play between them: power games to hide their own vulnerability, project it onto each other etc. The games twist and turn like a roller-coaster ride and sometimes one of the two will refuse to play, play counter, misread or try to undermine the game the other one has started as well as simply join in. In some ways it is the furthest I have gone from Philippe-type work in that it is a closely-scripted play based in text but it still uses all the pleasure of game-playing to make its points and hold the dramatic tension.

There are other techniques, as I said before which are rooted in pleasure but also worth discussing in their own right and which have strongly affected me. Rhythm and focus in particular.

Philippe teaches rhythm as a fundamental performance tool. Rhythm obviously isn't a new idea in theatre but it isn't often articulated in such a detailed way or related to performers so directly. I have found the way he uses it incredibly useful both as a performer and as a writer and a real key to enjoyment on stage. As a performer I learnt from him to develop a character from physical rhythm (which I now use in combination with other more "method" techniques.) I also learnt the fun of playing one rhythm against someone playing in another rhythm. I don't just mean slow or fast here, but all the subtle variations and physical and verbal manifestations that come once you begin to play with it and which is the basis not only of much comedy but also of dramatic tension. Extrapolating from the basic principle there is also the simple pleasure of doing something in a definite rhythm. For the first ten minutes of *Make Me a Statue* I stood on a pedestal and moved from one Rodin pose to another incredibly slowly. This would have been desperately boring had the performance energy of it not been one of great pleasure in moving my body that slowly for the audience. As it

Victoria Worsley as the commendatore in the finale of *Make Me a Statue* by Victoria Worsley and Caroline Ward. Photo: Dai Lewis.

was the audience frequently found it funny and often came out using words like "mesmeric". In my play *And All Because The Lady Loves ...* (which I also directed) the show opens with a door opening very slowly allowing light to spill out. As sleazy jazz music begins a woman steps through the door and walks down the steps into a spotlight at the front, all incredibly slowly. As soon as the actor moved without the pleasure of moving slowly it was nothing. As soon as she speeded up a bit it was nothing. When it was incredibly slow and when she clearly enjoyed that slowness it was very sexy and very exciting to watch. Simple but effective. This is a good case in point in fact. You can say to a performer "Open the door sexily and come down the stairs being sexy" and the result might well be a slightly embarrassed parody of sexy. If you say "Open the door and come on stage and walk down the steps all incredibly slowly and really enjoy how slowly and smoothly you can do it" the result will be something extremely sexy. You have to add focus into that mix as well but I'll come back to that.

There is also a crucial game to be found at the point when one performer finishes their "moment" and passes it to another, be that a piece of dialogue, or just an action or gesture. It is the essence of timing and Philippe is one of the few people to actually teach it as such. It is rooted in the pleasure of "passing the ball" and clarity of rhythm is needed to do it well. When a scene is not holding properly or feels unstructured or lifeless, it can come down to the actors not having clear enough rhythms and so not "passing the ball" clearly enough either, or failing into each other's rhythms and not finding the fun of playing against each other. Obviously that is not all there is to a performance but it is a very useful tool to help an actor express what they want and when isolated in this way can help to clear up problems and release a lot of creative possibilities. Again, actors can be resistant to this kind of method. They think you mean them to just play timing and nothing else. Obviously the heart, the emotions and the thoughts have to be there, but then skills of this kind are needed to express what is wanted otherwise the other work is utterly redundant. Most good actors have these kind of skills naturally but they are usually weak in one area or another and isolating techniques in this way can help if there are still problems when all the thoughts are in the right place as well as inspiring less obvious and more exciting ways of performing a piece. Equally importantly, real ensemble work cannot exist without each performer understanding and enjoying their place in the rhythm of the show as a whole at every moment. I have always found this kind of understanding of rhythm fundamental to my work.

Having learnt from Philippe to isolate rhythm as a factor down to the smallest detail of performance other aspects then became obvious: the rhythm of a set when it moves, of props that have to be used and of the lighting and how that affects a show and although I cannot discuss all these elements here, they are all things I think of when I write.

Indeed as a writer I think about rhythm all the time, both in terms of overall structure and shape of scenes and in terms of dialogue and character. I think of the rhythm games the actors could play on stage when I write even the most naturalistic dialogue. I love the strange rhythms of natural speech but I have also tried pushing rhythm games to see how much they can do. In *And All Because The Lady Loves …* I wrote three speeches on top of each other. Not a new idea but my theory was that if each one was written and performed in a very strongly different rhythm you would be able to hear all three. It almost worked. In Tattycoram we often had "split focus" pieces of this kind where all three of us did different things in different rhythms at the same time but they were less textual and more action-oriented and therefore easier for an audience to grasp. In my short piece *Lift and Separate* or *A Short Piece About Underwear*[4] I intercut five speeches very closely. The intercutting was for meaning as well as for rhythm but the rhythm is the key to make it work on stage. It is the different rhythms that distinguish the different characters and allow the audience to follow each one's thread as well as the element which holds the structure of the piece together. To pull it off the level of ensemble play between the five has to be very high indeed. Then there is the fun of sharing a rhythm and creating it together. This piece from *Night-Train* in which the couple think about going dancing is an example of applying that idea to a written text:

SAM	I take your
ANNA	Hand, I put my
SAM	Arm around my neck, I
ANNA	Slip your arm around my waist, and there's my foot
SAM	Inside my foot
ANNA	And my hip
SAM	Is next to mine.
ANNA	I feel your
SAM	Thigh
ANNA	Against my

SAM	Thigh.
ANNA	We step
SAM	Together, forward,
ANNA	Stop and turn
SAM	Our heads
ANNA	Sharply,
SAM	out
ANNA	And back
SAM	And stamp
BOTH	Together
	(Sharp intake of breath together)
ANNA	And glide
SAM	A step,
ANNA	Another step,
SAM	And again,
ANNA	Again,
SAM	One more.
ANNA	Stop, twist
SAM	And take
ANNA	My other hand, touch
SAM	My other cheek
ANNA	With mine,

SAM   Step,

ANNA   Step,

SAM   And step,

ANNA   And stamp.

                (Sharp intake of breath together)

ANNA   You spin me

SAM   Out and catch

ANNA   Me close, and snatch

SAM   Your hand, our stomachs pressed

ANNA   Together.

SAM   I place my leg

ANN   Between my

SAM   Legs and take another step

ANN   Together.

                (Sharp intake of breath together)

SAM   I twist you

ANNA   Out and let me

SAM   Fall backward on my knee. I have my

ANNA   Hand beneath my spine.

SAM   I can feel it through your

ANNA   Dress and we are drenched

SAM   In sweat.

ANNA   Our eyes

SAM   Blaze

ANNA   My hair is

SAM   Loose. My skin is

ANNA   Hot. My grip is

SAM   Firm. My neck is

ANNA   Smooth. My lips are

SAM   Close. My breath is

ANNA   (Whispers)… Edible.

Focus is another basic element which everyone uses but in isolating it Philippe offers you a fabulous tool. All it means is that the performer knows where their energy is focused. It can mean eyes in particular but it doesn't have to. An actor can focus all their energy in one direction while pointing their eyes in another. Focus gives a performer immediate direction and presence. Watching an actor walk across stage when they have no focus is like watching a lost, aimless person and that is probably how they feel. An actor with focus suddenly gives the audience a person with an intention and that is always more interesting to watch and better to perform. For example, ask someone to act sitting and thinking and often they will let their eyes wander and their energy disperse which becomes rapidly unwatchable, while in reality a person sitting thinking can be riveting to watch because their eyes and energy are usually completely focused even if that focus shifts.

Again isolating focus as a tool to play with allowed me to push the idea further. For example, it is also possible to focus an object and therefore draw the audience's attention to it, or to just a bit of an actor's body and let that bit communicate instead. That was a technique I pushed as far as I could in *And All Because The Lady Loves …* It was a play which looked at the effect of '40s Hollywood film images of women on women today and I wanted to achieve the effect of close-ups in the cinema. Obviously we couldn't zoom in and I couldn't shut the space down. We used light, but from a high lighting grid it is impossible to isolate just one hand in light and leave everything else completely black: there is too much spill. So, in combination with lights as tightly focused as possible and bounced off small mirrors etc., I worked with the actors to find a way to make the audience so interested in one hand taking a cigarette out of a box that they looked at nothing else. This you can do simply with focus. And to return to my old theme it needs pleasure. If the actor invites the audience to look at just their hand taking the cigarette out of the box because they love doing it with that focus, in that rhythm and they enjoy the cheekiness of asking the audience to go along with them, then the audience will buy it. If not, then they won't. Finally to come back to my woman opening the door and walking down the stairs at the top of the play – she needs to enjoy the slow rhythm but she also needs a strong focus. There is nothing more sexy than focus because it gives intention and everyone knows what that is.

These are just two of the tools that have affected how I work and which, by isolating them, I find immeasurably useful and creatively suggestive.

Philippe also teaches styles and I only have room to discuss one here, which is the one that has affected me most: **Melodrama**. Melodrama has been a dirty word although in recent years it has been rediscovered on the alternative scene, at least partly as a result of Lecoq and Gaulier. To my mind it is one of the most deeply pleasurable and expressive styles of all. Actors are on the whole terrified of the word melodrama with its connotations of ham and lack of truth but done well and kept light it is as truthful as any small piece of naturalism but more precise, more expansive, more generous. The pleasure is not in "sending it up" but in performing something highly charged with emotion as if your whole body is a beacon of light so that every blink of your eyelid can reach the back row of the gods. Melodrama after naturalism can be like playing the most serene piece of the Mozart Requiem after modern hymn tunes. It requires terrific skill to have that control but it also requires pleasure.

And All Because The Lady Loves … worked partly because performing 1940s film melodrama is so enjoyable. A performer could see it as simply problematic to talk over music and hold their head at the right angle to catch a beam of light on their left eye, but I worked hard with my cast to discover the huge pleasure there can be in speaking supported by a lush piece of Korngold music, in using the music to accentuate the text and playing games with the timing of it and how wonderful it is to create emotional effects by tilting your face in a beam of light and to play with which eye, which angle expresses what. This '40s melodrama is not what Philippe teaches but the basic skills are the same. (I also learnt a considerable amount from Neil Bartlett.) Most surprisingly though, I have found that the stillness, boldness and clarity which melodrama demands are qualities which are of great value in performing the smallest piece of "naturalism" as well.

I have only managed to cover a few aspects of Philippe's teaching here, but they are the aspects that have affected me most. In particular I have not had room to discuss Monika Pagneux's astonishing movement training. I am sure other of his students would find very different areas to talk about but one thing I am sure they would all agree is that although shouting it at you might not be the best way of teaching it, "Enjoy yourself for shit's sake" is crucially important advice.

Notes

1. *Make Me a Statue* was performed at the ICA and then on tour 1989–90.
2. *The Very Tragical History of Mary Shelley* was performed at the Edinburgh Festival and then on tour 1986/7. Other Tattycoram shows were 3 *Sisters in Oh! I Want to go to Moscow* which toured in 1987–8 and the solo show *Vesta Tilley* (1987).
3. And *All Because The Lady Loves* was performed at the Cockpit Theatre, as a Jade production hosted by Soho Theatre Company in June 1993.
4. *Lift and Separate* was a 15-minute piece commissioned by Soho Theatre Company and performed at the Cockpit Theatre as part of *(Small) Objects of Desire* in March 1993.

7

JOS HOUBEN: UNDERSTANDING
THE NEUTRAL MASK

Anthony Shrubsall

In the relationship between training and practice the actor is continually forced into a reassessment of the worth of the former in relation to the latter, the actor's present sense of self and way or mode of acting being invariably determined either in part or wholly by his past experiences. For the Lecoq trained actor this poses interesting questions particularly concerning the neutral mask and the activation of the state of neutrality in the actor; the significance and importance of which has been duly noted by Eldredge and Huston (1978), Felner (1985), and Frost and Yarrow (1990). Given that the neutral mask in Lecoq's teaching takes as its starting point the process of forgetting, 'erasing the psychological past in favour of a discovery of the immediate, physical present,' how does the actor arrive at this point? How does the actor locate himself physically in preparation for mask work? In what ways does he/she seek to realise the sense of economy so essential to the form? Can clarity of definition in movement be actively reconstituted in the moment? It is in seeking answers to these questions that Jos Houben has sought to integrate the practice, philosophy and teachings of Moshe Feldenkrais's 'Awareness Through Movement' programme into his own work on neutral mask as influenced by his training with Jacques Lecoq. Jos Houben qualified as a Feldenkrais teacher in 1994.

The following material is in two parts. The first part comprises of an analysis of a five-day workshop held under the auspices of the International Workshop Festival at the Theatre Workshop, Edinburgh, in September 1996. It was led by Jos Houben and entitled 'Doing is Understanding: The Neutral Mask'. It is not my purpose here to dutifully record everything that took place in the workshop but rather to select specific areas where the relationship between Feldenkrais and the neutral mask can be made explicit. The pattern for the work was very simple, entailing preparatory work through a series of Feldenkrais-based exercises followed by an exploration of the neutral mask individually and in groups. The relationship and connections between Feldenkrais training and the neutral mask were never elaborated upon throughout the workshop, instead one became conscious of a gradually evolving organic thread that linked the two together through the body of the participant, providing answers to the above questions concerning location, economy and clarity. The second part takes the form of an interview held with Jos Houben at the conclusion of the course.

Part One

In retrospect, the connections betweeen Feldenkrais and Lecoq's teaching of the neutral mask were there from the first morning of the workshop which began with a talk about the importance of receiving information from the horizontal position, i.e. lying down. A consideration of why the horizontal could be seen as a listening, resting, neutral place. Calming and soothing, but also potent. In this opening address Houben was quite clearly echoing Lecoq's own philosophy for the actor on the relationship between movement, stillness and space as expressed in an interview with Jim Hiley for *The Observer* in 1988:

You can't talk about movement unless you have equilibrium. You must know about the horizontal to undertake being vertical. What we give the public comes from within. There's a link, a reverberation betweeen inner and outer space. (p.40)

        In attending to this notion of the horizontal as a position of neutrality from a Feldenkrais perspective, the perception of neutrality is made physically concrete through the actual process of lying on the floor. Just as the mask has to locate and define itself through its relationship to space, the actor must locate and define the physical self through tactile experience. This physical sensation is then used to draw in one's own individual thoughts and feelings as one is encouraged to think and reflect upon the day and subsequently, the particular moment. The actor is thus encouraged to move from the individual thinking and feeling world of the real person to the immediate, instinctive physical world of the mask. The participant is then encouraged to find the neutral position through verbal direction, i.e. lying with hands placed palms down on the floor either side of the torso, legs uncrossed and feet outstretched, head facing directly towards the ceiling. A position which effectively unclutters the body of the actor and makes the body available, open and ready for meaningful movement not only outwards into space but also internally into the self of the actor. This drawing attention to the positioning of the body on the floor also marks the initiation of the sense of self-discipline required as the verbal directions issued never actually correct or remonstrate with the individual as regards one's position on the floor. Instead the instructions are carefully and quietly repeated, thus enabling the participant to achieve her/his own unique equilibrium or point of neutrality.

In the first exercises Houben drew attention to this notion of neutrality from both standing and lying positions, bringing to bear the Feldenkrais principle of scanning the state of the body through understanding the skeletal arrangement of the human being in both positions. Initially from standing and the exploration of weight transference by rotating the body through three points: front, back and sides, to lying down in the neutral position and drawing the feet up to standing position with the knees facing the ceiling. In this simple second movement the principles of economy and efficiency that were to subsequently feature in the following days were introduced. Again, the identification of three points was used to outline the structure of the movement Houben wished the class to follow: legs outstretched, feet drawn up with knees to sides, feet placed in standing position. The class was then invited to explore the reversal and stopping of that action. Inviting the discovery of economy and efficiency within such a simple action and locating that action in space through the human body's movement prior to the introduction of any mask work reinforced the simple truth that the mask exists only through the person wearing it, it has neither present nor future, only immediate present. As such the participants were encouraged to recognise the simplicity, functionality and inter-relationships between parts and whole in the potential of their own bodies before engaging with the mask itself.

This arrival at a potential state of neutrality was further compounded by an exploration of the neutral state and its extremes in the act of walking and running as the third component of pre-mask preparation. Finding an upright position judged from the crown of one's head and subsequently collapsing the body while walking, became running with weight forward, then back, noting the neutral position fleetingly between transitional states. This was given locational emphasis through the direction: 'to run with awareness of the space, floor, walls, light etc.' In essence returning us to the starting point of Feldenkrais's contemplation of the physical state, as determined by contact with the floor from the horizontal scanning exercise, although the body of the actor was now brought into a distinct relationship to space through movement.

The first example of actual mask work involved the the simple process of putting on the mask with one's back turned and turning to face the audience. Aiming to maximise the immediacy of the effect meant paying particular attention to the quality of turning and initiating that movement via the head. Having turned the mask must then respond to the instruction: 'Look to the horizon, scan the horizon', again initiating the action with the head not the eyes. There is a clear progression as the actor has used the exercise of scanning the body internally as a means of organising and identifying the material of his/her body in preparation for action. This now finds its outward expression, as the mask scans the space beyond the audience. Thus reiterating Lecoq's notion of the reverberation between inner and outer space referred to in the beginning. The importance of this action being led by the head is identified by Felner:

'As the eye represents the inner man, the neutral mask deflects the emphasis from the eye which is only barely visible, and places it instead on the movement of the head which is less generalised and less psychologically oriented. The audience perceives the movement of the head and not the eye.' (1985, p.158)

For the purpose of this exercise Houben suggested that the mask's eyes are effectively situated in the chest thus insisting on the importance of whole body engagement in the act of scanning. A placement that effectively helps to reduce or restrict extraneous movements that may distract from a whole body focus on the actor.

From the Feldenkrais maxim: 'We act in accordance with our self image' (1990, p.3) which entails the way a person holds their shoulders, head and stomach, voice and expression, stability and manner of presenting themselves, the process of 'turning' for the neutral mask becomes highly significant. According to Feldenkrais:

'Our image is formed through familiar actions in which approximation to reality is improved by bringing into play several of the senses that tend to correct each other. Thus, our image is more accurate in the region in front of our eyes than behind us or above our heads, and in familiar positions such as sitting or standing.' (1990, pp.22–3)

From this reading what Feldenkrais brings to the process of 'turning' for the neutral mask is a phenomenological sense of the mask's own self-image through the head of the actor as it leads the body in the actual act of 'turning'. This is made real as the self-image of the mask is kept in front of the eyes throughout the turn. If the direction of the eyes is separated from the mask then effectively the self-image of the mask is broken. When the reality of the individual actor's inability to concentrate intervenes to such an extent the mask ceases to exist at that precise moment.

Later in the workshop Houben used a specific exercise to assist participants in solving some of the problems experienced in the process of turning, particularly in terms of a loss of balance. This functional concrete application of Feldenkrais exercises was a consistent feature throughout the week. The exercise was approximately as follows:

'Lying on your back, raise your arms vertically and straight towards the ceiling. Raise one leg vertically. Explore twisting of pelvis from left to right. Link your head to the movement along with your arms. Send your arms and head in the opposite direction to your twisting pelvis. Explore the contrast between shoulders and pelvis. Listen to what your body tells you as a means of not overstretching and thus losing balance. Incorporate the use of your eyes in relation to other parts of your body. Send your eyes in one direction while your arms, leg and head travel in the opposite direction. Use both left and right sides for twisting and turning.'

The exercise works specifically to enable the individual to retain poise and control in the act of turning and twisting by creating additional freedom in one's movement. The incorporation of the eyes into the exercise and the deliberate playing with opposite directions is particularly interesting given the relationship of parts to whole in neutral mask work while the focus upon control over directional aspects of the body draws the body of the actor directly into the immediate, non-pyschological, physical world of the mask. The actor is thus made aware of the specific problem, i.e. control and balance in turning, and then consciously encouraged to correct it through a generalised approach via the exercise. The relationship between consciousness and awareness resonating between Feldenkrais practice and the mask is partly explained by Feldenkrais as follows:

'Awareness is consciousness together with a realisation of what is happening within it or of what is going on within ourselves while we are conscious.' (1990, p.50)

In addition to the work on turning, Houben also employed Feldenkrais techniques to walking and the neutral mask. This took three forms. In the first the Feldenkrais work involved floor exercises which began with lifting the head and then undulating the body through the pelvis to the head and then vice versa on both in and out breaths. This was then transferred to the upright position and participants were encouraged to explore the undulating sensation by pushing the different body parts outward into space using 'the bug' exercise.

'A bug drops to the floor in front of you and crawls towards you. It climbs up you from the foot to knee, then to your stomach, chest and nose before flying away and dropping to the floor in front of you to start the process all over again.'

Once the actors had become familiar with the physical experience they were then encouraged to apply the exaggerated movement to the act of walking beginning with the transference of weight onto one foot and then onto the other, thus creating the potential for 'commedia-style' walks leading onto character work. The second example of Feldenkrais merging into Lecoq picked up on problems encountered in the act of walking as the neutral mask. The approach was again to deal with the vertical problem horizontally. Actors were asked to lie on the floor as though standing and move their feet from toe to heel through a small action in the ankles.

A rolled towel was then placed under the neck and the actor rolled up and down over the towel in conjunction with the movement initiated from the ankles. This action was repeated with the towel placed under the shoulder blades and then the coccyx. Each time the actors were required to check their general physical state in relation to the floor at the completion of each stage in the exercise. For all participants the physical feeling of the floor became more solid in terms of their indentation or imprint on the floor. This change in the body's organisation was then monitored and observed through the identification of the body in space during the act of walking.

The third element also aimed to improve the quality of walking through the neutral mask but also interestingly directly applied to a particular session on mask and animals derived from mask and matter improvisations that are pure Lecoq. The Feldenkrais component again employed the horizontal in its administration. Participants were invited to lie on their backs, lifting their hips and shoulders alternately, then cross-laterally, observing the opposition between left and right (left shoulder, right hip and vice versa). They were then instructed to come to crawling first mono-laterally (left shoulder, left hip) then cross-laterally (left shoulder, right hip) on all fours and then, finally, to walking. In addition to focusing upon the rhythm essential to the neutral mask's walk (instinctively cross-lateral) it also prepared the actors for exploring the instinctive world of animals through movement. Given that the first animal improvisation involved the 'big cat', the work on crawling cross-laterally was directly beneficial in understanding the instinctive quality inherent to the movement of such animals.

The final aspect of Houben's workshop practice to be considered involves the workshop treatment of a classic Lecoq exercise for neutral mask: 'The Waking Up of the Giant'. This particular exercise serves to synthesise the various elements of Feldenkrais techniques used throughout the week. The exercise involves the mask asleep, it awakes, turns and stands in one movement, then walks forward defining and owning the space. The exercise begins in that most familiar Feldenkrais position, the horizontal. At the moment of awakening the mask must be immediately alert and instantly located to its surroundings. The process of turning and standing in one movement must be accomodated as smoothly, simply and efficiently as possible. Feldenkrais's notion of developing ideal paths of action through movement sum up this process for the mask:

'The ideal path of action for the skeleton as it moves from one position to another – say, from sitting to standing or from lying to sitting – is the path through which it would move if it had no muscles at all, if the bones were linked only by ligaments. In order to get up from the floor by the shortest and most efficient path, the body must be organised in such a way that the bones will follow the path indicated by a skeleton pulled up by its head. If they follow this path the muscular effort will be transmitted through the bones and all the effort of the pelvic muscles will be turned into useful work.' (1990, p.90)

Having stood up the mask then walks forward and defines the space through the gesture of space, bringing the arms up simultaneously from the sides to the chest, from where they fully extend outwards and apart in one smooth effortless gesture with palms and fingers outstretched. In the combination of this series of movements and gestures the actor must seek to execute them as economically and functionally as possible if one is to unlock the reality of the neutral mask's world. In extracting elements of the Feldenkrais method and applying them to the neutral mask, it appears that Jos Houben may well have found a key.

Bibliography

Eldredge, S. and Huston, H. (1978) 'Actor Training in the Neutral Mask', *The Drama Review*, vol.22, no.4, T-80.
Feldenkrais, Moshe (1977) *Awareness Through Movement*, Penguin.
Felner, Mira (1985) *Apostles of Silence*, Fairleigh Dickinson, Associated University Presses.
Frost, Anthony and Yarrow, Ralph (1990) *Improvisation in Drama*, Macmillan.
Lecoq, Jacques (1988) 'Moving Heaven and Earth', interview with Jim Hiley in *The Observer*, Sunday March 20th, p.40.

Part Two

I'd first like to ask you about the relationship between Feldenkrais and Lecoq that is obviously so important in your work and what you are creating from making links between the two.

There is no-one else that is doing such work at the moment, for me, the relationship between Feldenkrais and Lecoq, is me. As for the relationship between the two, I mix these two in my work because these are two very important, very influential teachings that I have had and that I wanted for myself. Lecoq has brought forth as well my wish to go deeper into understanding movement although that is not Lecoq's aim, both his movement training and his movement analysis have to do with theatre and space but for Feldenkrais it is a completely different thing altogether. It's more an educating of the senses of any human being. The discovery of how learning happens, how functioning develops and also how functions or ways of being in habits and habitual behaviour become stifled and imprisoned and repetitive. That's a danger to anything, to any way of living, to any life form and any performer. Now the link between the two is the human being and the understanding of how the human being works. The understanding of both Lecoq and Feldenkrais is in finding out what is not first of all, an artificial movement but a functional organic movement and both have gained this understanding from sport... and Lecoq, I guess, from his work as a physiotherapist. But also Lecoq from his interest in architecture and Feldenkrais being an engineer they are two very powerful men because they are thinkers and researchers at the same time as very practical people. They are both doers and makers, doers and fixers so they are thinking and they are doing, close together.

What does that create for the performer in relation to theatre do you think?

Well, first of all learning and teaching in terms of my performing is helped by me understanding better what learning and teaching is or can be. Secondly, maybe not so obviously the fact that more intimate and clear awareness of the self will produce a better flow of expressiveness. More spontaneity will also be an enormous help and that's what neutral mask for the theatre is all about. In a sense this works for every art form. It's a way of looking at the world, the neutral mask. It's a necessary passage. The passage to awareness through movement is more personal. Work which is an understanding of the person, of the self, and a clarifying of the self-image and so with both things if you want. The neutral mask being theatre is the state before anything happens and the self-image being the thing the actor plays with. Because he changes and transforms he plays with his self-image. He pretends to be other than himself and therefore needs thoughts feelings and movement to be expressive. That is the basic education of the two. Both meet and the neutral mask work is helped by this previous education, the clarity of the self.

You talk about the actor's problems, the functional concrete problems of locating oneself in space and organising oneself out of difficulties. Do you feel that this is an element that you are bringing together from the two practitioners in a clear linking to your own actual practice?

Yes. When you go somewhere you derive from something. You go on this creative journey and whenever you get lost or come to an end point you can return to nature or to daily life. There are all the things there and that's where we are as humans. We have to be non-judgemental and in Feldenkrais this non-judgemental attitude towards the self is very important. It means that in a certain moment judgements and opinions are necessary but we can also be free from them at a certain moment. We can go away and be free from what we learned and so we don't learn tricks or fixed ways of doing something. Once we've done them we can also chuck them out, throw them away. But where do you go to if you take somebody's mind training away, they're lost they're completely lost, you can't do that. You know what I mean, if you take somebody's smoking habit away they're lost unless it is replaced by something that you know is better or at least you bring them to a place of calm. That's what this neutral mask does and that's what this checking into the self does in Feldenkrais. You check into yourself again after this work, this pain this struggle, this emotion or whatever. The idea in Feldenkrais is can you recover? And the clearer the image of yourself, the quicker and the better you recover.

This is a very clear connection to the neutral mask isn't it? In terms of what the actor's capabilities are and the circle of influence that the mask operates within. The spatial dimension?

Yes, but it's very hard to debate that or talk about that theoretically because there is only one thing you can do – discover it through the neutral mask.

In terms of British theatre – you've had a long relationship with Complicité and British theatre in general has been exploring the dimensions of physicality in theatre for a while. Is there something that you think is missing in relation to the way that physicality seems to be a preoccupation?

I think that more than ever it's becoming part of the theatre. Certainly with Complicité, with Steven Berkoff. These people have brought the gesture and the movement and rhythm of a text back to the theatre. Not that many people did that instinctively but there's a sort of basic problem in English theatre for me which is in design. This is not generalised, not made clear that the space you're in involves the function of the body, of the actor rather because what is the body? I mean that is so deeply rooted, these artificial divisions we make which are language divisions which are useful but we unfortunately start to live them as well. And these in our own bodies. So I see in design and even costume-making a bigger problem than in performing. In performing I see great performers and I see directors with new stuff and it's all very good but design tends to be aesthetic or, especially in Britain, pure illustration. It's a visual school of illustration and not of space, that's what I feel. My experience with designers is that they understand concept and image but not so much space because they don't move themselves. Get them on the floor with the neutral mask and you'll get much more exciting designs or spaces. Space can be like a mask, a movable living thing where vertical and horizontal are understood as being the true parameters of any derivation or any change. An impossible unemotional space can change according to the light or the place of the actor in it and I find far too many of these designs are self-conscious and attract too much attention to detail. The best spaces you see for theatre are German and Italian; they are my architects, they are my designers who understand space. For me the German theatre has a sense of the monumental and of course you must include Peter Brook where the space comes from the actor.

In relation to when you are making a performance, when you're creating a piece, what sort of material attracts you?

That's interesting. I'm attracted by many many things but I go towards that corner usually where I feel there's not enough happening and for the last year that has been the real slapstick, physical burlesque. I've missed it and it gives great joy and there's a way to deal with violence and with all the negativeness, the clumsiness, the stupidity of human behaviour and still an audience can watch it from a distance and connect with it through laughter. I find it fascinating. Destabilisation you can do through laughter which allows you to see and recognise and I'm very fascinated by that. I'm fascinated by the moment, I see companies bring successful work and I don't want to be them when I see the work of Brook. I don't want to do that then. That already fires my imagination and my own experiences with my own teaching and my own learning with ... for example, the regular workshops I do or the shows I see, I learn from them. Even the Feldenkrais method in which every person I touch as a Feldenkrais practitioner teaches me something. That is somehow waking up something very unclear at the moment about the nature of art itself and sensitivity to rhythm and music to do with this very intimate contact with the self. I worked on a poem which was about an environment with a writer in this way.

What was the name of it?

Beloved Earth/Beloved Land. A tale of a migrating bird crashing down on a stone. It crashes down in the neighbourhood of a sort of area where this land-living creature lives and its hole, its nest has blown away as well and they're exposed. They could be each other's food and one is a woman dressed as a woman and one is a man in a suit yet he moves like a bird. There they are, they look at each other. At night this bird sings about this country he goes to, his wings are broken but she knows how to walk on the terrain. She teaches him to walk and swim if he keeps his orientation together ... the whole thing was text and movement.

Did you make connections with neutral mask in the show?

Absolutely, the whole approach of that show was to do with mask. Which I love doing and which was, I mean it wasn't really French or English in fact it has never been performed in France. It has been performed in Belgium but never in France. It has been performed in England as well but you don't tour for long with a French show. The ambition was that this French text should touch the audiences by the quality of the words and the silences that were between them and it worked. People were electrified. So these are the experiments and I carry that into something else. The show is finished now and I can't revive that again so I must think what is the next step?

Is there something in relation to the Lecoq training that you go back to regularly?

Constantly. The way that training works it keeps on nourishing you and I know how to nourish myself from it. I have not learned exterior things: I've learned many interior things that I can clarify till the end. I need five lives to clarify it and I share that when I talk to Simon McBurney and to other colleagues who work in the same way. Only recently we worked together in July in Paris and we were saying how we were profiting from certain things again from the school and how it's amazing that such things will return. It was as if only now we saw what powerful things they were. Only now. It's very moving because we went straight back to the first week of the school and we were loving it. Saying 'That's it!' It is the same with this week-long workshop that we did here.

You mentioned yesterday about Complicité and how you thought it was such a good thing that they were failing with Foe.

Yes, but is it a failure? Is it for the audience? For the actors maybe and for many theatres and for maybe the Arts Council? It is clearly at some moment but in Sweden or Switzerland it was seen as the most amazing thing because they saw it for the first time. They were not comparing it with anything because they had not seen Complicité's work before. But it will certainly be very instructive and instrumental to Complicité absolutely. It is important that the most terrible thing that can happen, the most important thing we all have, which is awful when it gets taken away, is our right to fail and our necessity to fail. If that is taken away then we are not free anymore.

Does Lecoq give you, even encourage that?

Absolutely. If it is anything, it is a school for freedom and freedom from success as well.

Thank you.

8

AFTERWORD

Ralph Yarrow

"Celui qui invente le langage, ce n'est pas moi."

Artaud is talking about written language here. And saying that its preexistent forms condition the everyday persona, which can only take them on reluctantly and which in so doing gets the feeling that it is somehow losing touch with the real 'me'. Language in this sense is the property of others, it defines you in spite of yourself, it says what you don't want it to. Beckett knows all about this. Lecoq's Artaudian addition is to suggest that 'celui qui invente le langage du geste, ça peut bien être moi', which is to say that the impulse to movement comes from a less socially-conditioned locus; but even though Bim Mason recalls what is presumably a Lecoq claim that interaction and response in theatre is best generated viscerally, Lecoq is not only concerned with involuntary affective experience. The neutral mask work, as John Martin lucidly glosses it and as Simon Murray describes it, moves performers to a level *from which* formulation is possible, but which in some sense underlies any recognised emotional or intellectual content. The *moi* that is discovered in the mask is more that of Valéry than of Artaud, it is a potential in waiting, an impetus to action. Somewhere from here languages are invented (Lecoq says students "(apprennent) à inventer des langues"). I don't know how much Martin (or Lecoq) are echoing Luce Irigaray, but his title recalls hers in *Ce sexe qui n'en est pas un (This sex which is not [yet] one)* and thereby her sense that what remains to be articulated is precisely what the (masculist) Symbolic Order has not covered, what is as yet unsaid, what lives in the domain of silence. Like Roland Barthes' notion of the "texte scriptible", something created in the interplay and excitement generated between writer, reader and artefact, Lecoq's *autocours* and his resolute refusal to do it for his students and insistence that they become actor/authors gives the participant the chance to buck the system (as Martin rightly perceives in his delight at disagreeing with Lecoq). System there must be, or there is no structure to learn from; and systems are always potentially authoritarian. But in spite of doubts expressed in some of the essays, perhaps Lecoq's profoundest gift is precisely the ambiguity and the danger of "doing what you do". Only a theatre which can, however briefly, return to a state before languages and stand amazed at its own potential can, as Shakespeare knew, really start the business of reform. The second step in that business is learning to write in whatever way and to fight the sterility of the already said and done; that you have to do anyway, wherever you start from. You might as well (just as well) go the whole hog and begin from the beginning.

"We are trying to understand a human ground which is different from ours."[1]

In order to create a theatre which does not yet exist it is necessary to enter into the possibility of a different symbolic form (Schiller calls the ability to do this *Formtrieb*, the impulse to form; he says it rests upon and is expressed through *Spieltrieb*, the impulse to play.) The language(s) of theatre have to be reinvented. If Artaud was after this so is Lecoq.

You can only enter the possibility of a different symbolic system if you get out of the one you are in and understand its arbitrariness; if you are able to suspend its schemes of making sense and see them as a kind of 'magic if.' That, most fundamentally, is the function of neutrality and is a hazardous business and it may not, in fact almost certainly will not, 'make sense' to those who only think in the old one. Artaud was not the only artist to feel the results, excluded from the world of 'sense' as defined by the extant norms. De Nicolás, in the book referred to, is proposing that in order to understand the *Rig Veda*, it is necessary to reconstruct the system proposed by its language and its language alone: not that of later commentators or other philosophical positions. Its language, however, is essentially one of *chanted hymns*, whose meaning cannot be reduced to statements about their content, but has to be grasped by moving onto the "shifting, resounding, evanescent, vibrating and always sounding silence of the *musical* world on which the Rig Veda stands" (de Nicolás, p. 11). That doesn't sound too odd as a description of the kind of 'mime' produced by Lecoq. Only through this essentially deconstructive attitude towards the familiar can the as-yet-unknown be entered into. The methodology for doing so is central to Lecoq's practice, but it is not generally practised. The work which arises may itself tend – just like Brechtian or other forms of artistic defamiliarisation – to offer ways in over a period of time. The performers have first to access the impulse to play, and then teach it to their audiences. Not surprisingly, there will initially be some sense of strangeness; and the 'product' may not appear to fit the mould of what was previously considered comprehensible.

Play is what links Lecoq and Gaulier most centrally. There are some differences in their emphasis and focus (Gaulier says he hasn't got a system and suspects Lecoq of having one; he uses the *bouffon* for perhaps more aggressively subversive purposes than Lecoq, rather as Fo uses farce more aggressively than Strehler; he plays the role of lugubrious and long-suffering pedagogue as opposed to Lecoq's slightly distant mystagogue). But both are in tune with Schiller's awareness that the spirit of invention is the spirit of play, and that these are fundamental human resources which can counter the deadliness of pompous art. The reason, most profoundly, is that play is play with the system and play out of the system: it changes the name of the game at will, and is the will to go on changing its name and its form. It is also what unites players, whether on or off the stage, because it gives them a stake in the game, it affirms the complicity of being able to change the way it is. It theatre can go on doing that, it (and we) may survive.

Note

1. Antonio de Nicolás, *Meditations through the Rig Veda*, Shambhala, Boulder & London 1978, p. 13

9

LECOQ TALK

David Gaines

Wherever theatre people go they gather round to talk;
And nowadays it's 'de rigueur' to drop the name 'Lecoq'.

What is the deal, that people feel the need to hire henchmen
To do a job of slandering the students of this Frenchman?

It's not as if he's hatched a plot to flood this island nation
With groups of clone-like slaves to his demonic inspiration.

But people cry 'Lecoq!' like demagogues cry 'the economy!'
In lamentations that divide the theatre's one-time bonhomie.

Are we our brother's keeper? Is it our fault that he's boring?
Can we be held to task because the audience is snoring?

For God's sake no! Let credit go where credit should be due;
And do not blame the teacher for what pupils don't, or do.

For what these groups that call themselves 'Lecoq-based' share between
them
Is only that they need a book for those who haven't seen them.

And who among us hasn't needed that in early days –
When eager, young, and desperate to bring the world our plays?

So yes, their show may disappoint, and well you may decry it,
But if you think it's easy to be brilliant, you should try it.

You come with expectations and demands and find them wanting,
No wonder their performance is impaired – it can be daunting.

And anyway, perfection loses much of its felicity
When genius doesn't shine through a surprise of serendipity.

It's not like at the florists, where each bloom's a perfect fit;
To grow the living flowers you must trundle in the shit.

So don't bemoan your poor backside, and all your arteries hardening,
You too must play your part in our 'complicité' of gardening.

NOTES ON CONTRIBUTORS

Franc Chamberlain is Senior Lecturer in Performance Studies at University College Northampton and series editor for *Contemporary Theatre Studies* and *Contemporary Theatre Review*.

John Martin trained at the Ecole Jacques Lecoq and performed with companies such as La Mama ETC (New York), Stockholm City Theatre, and the Arts Theatre London before founding Pan Project, an Intercultural Performance Ensemble, in 1986. He has an exceptional knowledge of world performance traditions, has directed over fifty productions worldwide, and taught the UK's first ever course in non-western theatre techniques and their accompanying philosophies at Goldsmith's College, University of London. Recent productions in the UK created with artists such as Peter Badejo and Mallika Sarabhai have centred on contemporary women's issues (*Shakti, Sita's Daughters*) and the dangers of social manipulation in traditional storytelling (*Itan Kahani*).

Bim Mason attended the Ecole Jacques Lecoq from 1983–85. He is director of Circomedia, The Academy of Circus Arts and Physical Theatre based in Bristol. As a freelance director he has worked with companies such as Talking Pictures (with whom he won a Fringe First Award at the Edinburgh festival in 1989), Welfare State International and Peepolykus. He created and performed with Mummer&Dada (1985–90) and a book, *Street Theatre and Other Outdoor Performance*, was published by Routledge in 1992.

Simon Murray (stage name for Simon Henderson) is Senior Lecturer in Performance Studies at the University College of Ripon and York St. John. Until 1995, and when this article was written, he was a director, performer and teacher working largely in the field of physical theatre. In 1986, after 15 years working in higher and adult education and as a trade union officer, he went to Paris to study acting and movement with Philippe Gaulier and Monika Pagneux. He is currently undertaking postgraduate research on the sociology of British physical theatre(s) in the Theatre Studies department of Lancaster University. Simon is also a director of Cleveland Theatre Company.

Anthony Shrubsall is a Lecturer in Drama and Performance Studies at University College Northampton. Following a rather diverse and varied career as a Special Education teacher in both England and the USA. He received his MA with Distinction from Royal Holloway, University of London in 1991. Prior to taking up his current post he was dramaturg to Laurence Boswell at the Gate Theatre in London for the 1993 production of Ramón del Valle-Inclán's *Bohemian Lights*. His research interests include the theatres of Brecht and Meyerhold, contemporary political theatre, and 'labyrinth' performance work.

Victoria Worsley writes and performs her own work as well as doing a wide variety of acting work in theatre, film and TV. She is artistic director of a new production company, JADE, which presents new work that combines the written text with a visual/physical approach.

John Wright was co-founder of Trestle Theatre Company and, until 1992, co-directed most of their repertoire including *Top Storey, Ties That Bind*, and *State of Bewilderment*. Outside Trestle, his credits include: *Circus Moon* (Half Moon Theatre), *Master Peter's Puppet Show* and *The Overcoat* (Tottering Bipeds). *Aesop – A New Opera* (Royal Opera House and National Youth Music Theatre) won a Fringe First at the Edinburgh Festival in 1991. *On The Verge of Exploding* (The John Wright Co.) was nominated for an Independent Award (1993) and *She'll Be Coming Round the Mountain* (Back Stairs Influence) won the Guardian International Student Drama Award (1994).

   John is an international teacher of theatre, a regular contributor to the work of the Royal National Theatre Studio and The Actors' Centre, and is course leader for the BA in Acting course at Middlesex University where he is a Principal Lecturer.

Ralph Yarrow is Senior Lecturer at the University of East Anglia where he teaches drama, European literature and French language. He has directed and performed in India and the UK and in English, French and German; his writing includes adaptations for the stage. He has written on the theory and practice of improvisation, on contemporary literary and dramatic theory, on consciousness and aesthetics; his directing work includes Kokoschka, Jarry, Różewicz, Churchill, Daniels, Pinter and Vinaver. He is currently writing a book on Indian theatre.

INDEX

Other titles in the Contemporary Theatre Studies series:

Other titles in the Contemporary Theatre Studies series: